Praise for Human Gifts

"For me, this book is where esoteric theology meets the practical world of everyday life. A wonderful read for daily inspiration in how to lead the good life."

—Dr. T. J. W., HISTORIAN/AUTHOR

"James Hallam's inspiring words will leave you wanting to wake up each day with passion and purpose. Truly a great read that will touch your heart and thinking. I purchased several for gifts."

—CHERYL ECTON, CEO ELITE BUILDING SERVICES

"What is the hope for our broken world, for our own brokenness? *Human Gifts* provides us hope. Hope that we can live a life of meaning. Hope that by sharing our gifts of empathy, generosity, compassion, and more— we can be a healing force for ourselves and the world. *Human Gifts* is beautifully written, compelling, wise, thought-provoking, and humbling. It has inspired me to search my soul and to live my journey differently. It is a must read for all."

—KAREN PALMER, ATTORNEY

"*Human Gifts* touched my heart in a way like no other book has done. The impact of this book on my mind caused an immediate goal of my wanting to be a kinder and giving person. Highly recommend this book for all ages. Never too early or late to touch a life."

—Sara Canuso, Women That Influence

"*Human Gifts* touches one's soul at the core. It challenges me to live each day thinking about how I can encourage and lift up those around me in order to make their lives better! Especially in challenging times, it is a 'must read'."

—Henry Winchester, Executive Director,
Elite Building Services

Human Gifts

Giving to Transform Ourselves, Others, and the World

JAMES R. HALLAM

Hailyn Enterprises

Published by:
Hailyn Enterprises
WILMINGTON, DE

Copyright © 2022 James R. Hallam

ISBN-13: 979-8-9856872-2-4

Editorial consultation
Jennifer Hallam

Cover and interior
Gary A. Rosenberg • www.thebookcouple.com

Printed in the United States of America

Contents

*For the church members and students who have given
me the gifts of listening, presence, and affirmation.*

*They have taught me more than I could
ever teach them.*

Introduction

I have been sitting here at my desk thinking about what it means to be a Christian in such a confusing, conflicted, and dark time as our society and world is currently experiencing. For so many, to be Christian requires no more than verbalizing a statement of faith and following traditional rules. It seems to me, however, that this understanding is antiquated, and frankly, insufficient for meeting our moment. The essence of Christianity is not to be found in the singing of hymns, the recitation of scripture, the forcefulness of prayer, or the repetition of creeds. Rather, I believe that our responsibility and accountability as Christians today is centered in Jesus of Nazareth and founded in praxis. It is only through our *actions* that we make real the love of Christ that has the potential to transform the world. Our challenge, our promise, and our hope, therefore, lie in our commitment to walking the way of Jesus, following his example, internalizing his lessons, and living gospel values.

I write this book not only for people, including me, who seek to be conduits of God's presence, but also for anyone who wants to make a difference and live a life of meaning. Each of us, whether or not we affiliate with a religious institution or affirm a creative, powerful force beyond ourselves, has a divine spark within us; we are born with certain capacities that, when nurtured, can actuate our best selves, enrich the lives of others, and bring wholeness and healing to a broken earth. These capacities are the essence of our humanity, what I will refer to throughout this book as our "human gifts."

I encourage all of us, regardless of belief or background, to consider the personhood and life of Jesus because Jesus, in his humanity, was an individual who not only realized these innate capacities fully but also shared them generously. If we can isolate and embrace the attitudes and behaviors of Jesus that inspired hope, light, change, and celebration in the world, then we, too, can say that we made the most of our precious human gifts.

Several years ago, while in a department store, I casually looked in a case that held an array of necklaces. A fire opal caught my eye. Sparkling under the bright lights of the jewelry display, it was beautiful. I imagined how lovely it would look hanging on a gold chain around my wife's neck. I checked the price. Wow, too expensive! I walked away that day, but on several occasions when I returned to the store, I felt compelled to visit the necklace. Finally, after viewing it for the fourth time (and discovering it was on sale), I gave in and bought it. It was, I thought, a gift worthy of the beautiful person my wife is. She deserved it.

At some point, we have all given a gift. In fact, I think it is fair to suggest that most of us have spent considerable time thinking about the perfect gift for someone special to us, and even more time purchasing or making, boxing and wrapping that gift. Gift-giving is a human phenomenon, and in our society, we have no want for occasions to give—birthdays, anniversaries, baby showers, Christmas, Hanukkah, and Valentine's Day to name just a few.

There is no doubt that material gifts have impact on those who receive them. Think about the sheer joy of a child opening a present and exclaiming, "It's what I always wanted!" or the warm smile of a new neighbor receiving a welcome basket. Gifts are a way of letting others know that we are thinking of them, that we care about them and appreciate them; they indicate our willingness to invest time, effort, and dollars in their happiness or comfort.

But this book is not about the gift of things.

I would have you contemplate a different kind of gift. Gifts without price tags. Gifts without limits or measure. Gifts that we can give every day, in any time, place, or circumstance, be it one of joy or sorrow, health or pain, orientation or disorientation. These are the innate gifts we have to be lights in the midst of darkness, to bring love in the midst of hate, and to help hurting brothers and sisters experience the transformative powers of acceptance and understanding in a culture which too often denigrates vulnerability and discounts the value of each human being. What I am talking about are gifts of shared humanity.

The truth is, when we give human gifts, we can make a greater difference in the lives of others than we can with any packaged present. What's more, when we share of ourselves, we come to know a satisfaction unrivaled by the good feelings that come from giving even the most glittering of opal necklaces.

Many years ago when I was a campus minister, I had stationery at the top of which was a quote by Baron Von Hugel, the Roman Catholic philosopher and author. As he was dying, he called his niece to his bedside. She heard him breathe his last words: "Caring is everything; nothing matters but caring." It is my firm conviction that we are only fulfilled as people when we seek to touch the lives of others with kindness, generosity, respect and love. We ultimately find meaning not in what we get but in what we give.

This book is not a theoretical one but a practical one. It is intended to help you explore your own innate capacities—your gifts—so you can, in disciplined fashion, realize and amplify them in your daily living.

The format is not very complicated. Each chapter will focus on one particular human gift. For each, I will share commentary from others who have found it significant, relevant passages from scripture, and some thoughts about how you might cultivate the seed of that gift within yourself and share it more freely with the world. To make the discussion more substantive and real, I will also be including autobiographical material that speaks to my own personal experiences on both the giving and receiving end of each gift. Don't be surprised to find that few, if any, of the gifts are mutually exclusive—the qualities and characteristics associated with each overlap and are often integrated.

Finally, and importantly, every chapter will conclude with some questions for further reflection and action. These questions are the key to getting the most out of the book. There is no saint among us. Part of our efforts as people walking the Jesus way is to reflect on our behavior and acknowledge that at times it is antithetical to the wisdom of the master teacher. Once we have completed an honest and authentic self-inventory we will be more equipped to make choices that will result in personal change. It is a process that requires motivation, intention, and courage. Find comfort in remembering that change does not happen overnight; the opportunity to evolve as Jesus people is ours until the day we die.

Before moving on with the task just described, I want to acknowledge the many special people who have showed me by example how to walk the Jesus way. We all learn through observing what others say and how they live. Those who have had the biggest impact on me have been relational people, people who have been congruent in their witness to what really matters in life. I have experienced grace, the very essence of the divine, from beloved family members, teachers, friends and numerous church members. Thanks be to God for each of them and especially for my soulmate, my wife Kerry, who has shared with me the most cherished gift of unconditional love.

CHAPTER 1

The Gift of Love

"Darkness cannot drive out darkness: only light can do that. Hate cannot drive out hate: only love can do that."
—Martin Luther King Jr.

"Love has no age, no limit, and no death."
—John Galsworthy

"Ultimately love is everything."
—M. Scott Peck

Throughout fifty-five years of ministry, I have been an unwavering advocate of love. In fact, I remember a person in one of the churches I served suggesting that I talked too much about it. Really? I submit that one can never talk enough about love! After all, you can, as Paul asserts in Corinthians, have all the material things in the world, but if you do not have love, you have nothing. Without love, we are bankrupt.

Over the decades, I have performed countless marriages and funeral services. Time and again on these occasions, I have read Paul's beautiful hymn on love:

Love never gives up.
Love cares more for others than for self.
Love doesn't want what it doesn't have.
Love doesn't strut,
Doesn't have a swelled head,
Doesn't force itself on others,
Isn't always me first,
Doesn't keep score of the sins of others,
Doesn't revel when others grovel.
Takes pleasure in the flowering truth,
Puts up with anything,
Trusts God always,
Always looks for the best,
Never looks back,
But keeps going to the end.
Love never dies.

Paul ends his commentary with these words: "Trust steadily in God, hope unswervingly, love extravagantly. And the best of the three is love." (I Corinthians 13:1-8 TM). What an awesome statement Paul makes. His verses give substance to the abstract idea of love and encourage love as a way of life.

Love is not an option for the person claiming to be Christian. Love is the grounding, the bedrock if you will, of a Christian ethic, the core of Christian understanding and living. Reflect on the wisdom of Jesus when asked which was the most important commandment by a religious scholar. His answer:

The first in importance is, "Listen, Israel: The Lord your God is one; so love the Lord God with all your passion and prayer and intelligence and energy." And here is the second: "Love others as well as you love yourself. There is no other commandment that ranks with these." (Mark 12:28-31 TM)

Jesus mandates love as the way to make God alive in the world. As the writer of John informs us, love defines the very essence of God. "My beloved friends," he exhorts, "let us continue to love each other. No one has ever seen God, ever. But if we love one another, God dwells deeply within us, and his love becomes complete in us—perfect love." (1 John 4:7-8 TM). He continues in a later passage:

God is love. When we take up permanent residence in a life of love, we live in love and God lives in us. . . If anyone boasts, "I love God," and goes right on hating his brother or sister, thinking nothing of it, he is a liar. If he won't love the person he can see, how can he love the God he can't see? The command we have from Christ is blunt: Loving God includes loving people. You've got to love both. (1 John 4:17, 20-21 TM)

But what does it mean for the Christian person—or any person—to love?

I cannot tell you the number of times I have heard an individual eulogized at a memorial service as a "loving person." I'm sure that means different things to different people. But I subscribe to Carl Michalson's notion that love is not about a feeling. As Michalson, the theologian referred to as "Mike" by the students at Drew Theological School, writes, "The essential thing is not to feel love, but to do love. We do not feel then act; we act, then we feel."[1] To be a loving person in this sense is to demonstrate love in our actions towards others. Love involves respect and high regard for all people. It is a chosen attitude manifested in overt behavior.

For the recipient, the gift of love can be transformational. A story from *Chicken Soup of the Soul* stands out to me as an undeniable testament to this creative power of love. As the author tells us, a college professor has his sociology class go into an underserved, low-income neighborhood in Baltimore to get case histories of 200 young boys. Without exception, the evaluation of each boy's future was: "He hasn't got a chance."

Twenty-five years later another sociology professor revisited the project, asking his students to follow up on those boys. Twenty of the original group had moved away or died. Of the remaining 180 students, it was discovered that 176 were living as successful professionals—lawyers, doctors and businessmen. The professor was stunned and decided to interview all the men still in the area. "How do you account for your success?" he asked. Each of the men replied, emotionally, "There was a teacher." The professor located the teacher and asked her what magic formula she had used to overcome the disadvantages they faced. She said with a twinkle in her eye and a smile on her lips: "It was really quite simple. I loved those boys."[2]

We often think about love in terms of another person. Someone gives us the gift of love or we give it to them. But there is another equation to consider. Jesus mandates that not only are we to love God and each other, but we are also to love ourselves. We are to acknowledge and know that we are worthwhile, valuable, and special. I recall listening to a tape by Brian Tracey in which he suggests an antidote to poor self-esteem. Stand in front of a mirror fully seeing yourself and exclaiming, "I love myself! I love myself." As I view my wrinkled face and excessive weight, this affirmation makes me laugh. It does, however, send a positive message to my psyche. Sound psychology suggests that if I have a negative view of myself, I cannot authentically love another person.

A person of faith affirms that God sustains, comforts, and challenges and is experienced as the divine presence in the interior space of all humans. We know God as the divine spark giving life and wholeness. We are able, if we open our hearts, to receive the eternal gift of love. If we choose to do so, we can give this gift to others.

I am unapologetically a follower of Jesus of Nazareth. Why? Because I believe his message of love is the way that enables us to live the most abundant life. Because I believe that love of God, self, and others connects us to each other and enables us to live our dash—our moment in time—making real the heart of the universe. As we love each other we are part of the eternal flow which births us and, in the end, unites us to the source of all things.

The circle is a symbol embraced by many religious traditions to suggest simplicity, wholeness, perfection, and the cyclical nature of life. For the Christian, the circle connotes the love of God, which has neither beginning nor end. I suggest that the circle is also a fitting paradigm for thinking about love as a human gift. Love is the nourishing element, the rich soil if you will, that feeds all of our other innate capacities—compassion, empathy, acceptance, forgiveness, and the rest. At the same time, love is the splendiferous tree that grows from those roots. The gift of love is both the origin and the outcome.

This line from a hymn, *The Gift of Love,* touches my spirit: "Though I may speak with bravest fire, and have the gift to all inspire, and have not love, my words are vain, as sounding brass and hopeless gain."[3] We can live to the fullness of our humanity only as we receive and give the gift of love.

Give the gift of love. It is the greatest gift we can give.

Reflections Reflections

+ What does love mean to you? Do you feel loved?

+ Who do you find it difficult to love? Why? Do you want to do something about it?

+ How can we love in a world of so much hate, suffering and injustice?

The Gift of Kindness

"Three things in human life are important.
The first is to be kind. The second is to
be kind. And the third is to be kind."

—HENRY JAMES

"You cannot do a kindness too soon for you
never know how soon it will be too late."

—RALPH WALDO EMERSON

"Imagine what our real neighborhoods would
be like if each of us offered, as a matter of course,
just one kind word to another person."

—FRED ROGERS

Mr. Tushman is the principal of the fictional Beecher Prep Middle School in R.J. Palacio's heartwarming novel, *Wonder*. In the book, Tushman gives a commencement address to the fifth and sixth grade graduates in which he quotes a line from the pages of J. M. Barrie's *The Little White Bird*: "Shall we make a new rule of life…always to try to be a little kinder than is necessary?"

The principal explains that he loves the line because it reminds him "that we carry with us, as human beings, not just the capacity to be kind, but the very choice of kindness." Kindness, he goes on to tell the students, is expressed through simple acts, but has a huge impact:

If every single person in this room made it a rule that wherever you are, whenever you can, you will try to act a little kinder than is necessary—the world really would be a better place. And if you do this, if you act a little kinder than is necessary, someone else, somewhere, someday, may recognize in you, in every single one of you, the face of God.[1]

Wow. That's powerful stuff.

I love the speech that Palacio has written for Tushman because it resonates so deeply with my own beliefs. All human gifts live within us from the moment we are born, but developing those gifts fully and sharing them freely requires intention. As a result of our thoughtful choices and deliberate behavior, our divine potential is made manifest.

But let's get back to kindness, specifically.

The idea that kindness can effect real change is not just a conjecture; it is validated by science! Kelli Harding, in *Live Longer, Happier and Healthier with the Groundbreaking Science of Kindness,* describes a 1978 study on the relationship between high blood cholesterol and heart health. Over several months, a group of New Zealand white rabbits were all fed the same high fat diet. As expected, when tested, the cholesterol values were high in all of the rabbits. All seemed destined for a heart attack and possible stroke. The expectation was that all the rabbits would show fatty deposits on the inside of their arteries as well. So, when Dr. Robert Nerem, the lead researcher, examined the rabbits' tiny blood vessels, he was stunned. One group of rabbits had 60 percent fewer deposits than the others. How could this be? It was truly a medical mystery.

Dr. Nerem knew there could be things in the protocol that were not taken into account and were not a part of the research design. As it turned out there was a postdoc who had recently joined the team. She was, according to Nerem "an usually kind and caring individual." All the animals with fewer deposits were under her care. Upon investigation, it was discovered that the postdoc handled the rabbits differently. She fed them, talked to them, petted them, and gave them love. The study was repeated, this time with care of the rabbits as an intentional variable. The results were the same.

What was the conclusion of the researchers? "These studies," they wrote, "indicate something is missing in the traditional biomedical model. It wasn't diet or genetics that made a difference in which rabbits got sick and which stayed healthy; it was kindness." Or, as Kelli Harding summarizes it, "what affects our health in the most meaningful ways has as much to do with how we treat one another, how we live, and how we think about what it means to be human than with anything that happens in the doctor's office."[2] This phenomenon is now referred to as the "Rabbit Effect."

Jesus understood the Rabbit Effect intrinsically. Kindness was fully incorporated into his lifestyle. He touched a man with leprosy, whom others considered "untouchable," and healed him. He raised the dead son of the widow in Nain, lest she be left destitute. When he met the woman with a questionable reputation at the well, he gave her hope. While his disciples rebuked the parents who brought their children to him for blessing, Jesus welcomed them. "Let these children alone," the teacher said, "Don't get between them and me. These children are the kingdom's pride and joy." (Luke 18:15-17 TM)

I will never forget a young woman who volunteered at the People's Emergency Center, a weekend homeless shelter for families, single women and youth that I co-founded in 1972. Karen, a nurse by profession, embodied the behavior Jesus taught. There was another woman, Sylvia, who was chronically homeless and came often to the PEC. She was known to many by the derogatory nickname the "duck woman" because of a quacking sound she made. Sylvia also had a terrible shake, which we assumed was a symptom of Parkinson's disease.

One day Sylvia came in while Karen was doing a volunteer shift. Karen led her to the shower, helped her bathe, combed her hair, and got her some clean clothes. She brought Sylvia into the dining area, got her a plate of food, sat at the table with her and held her wrist to steady her shaking hand. With encouraging words, she helped Sylvia eat. "You can do this," Karen said, "you can do this." The gift Karen gave Sylvia was not complicated; it was not expensive or extravagant. Karen simply treated Sylvia as a human being worthy of dignity and respect. She gave her the gift of kindness, and it made a difference.

Another story of kindness that strikes me as worthy of Jesus's model is one that my wife tells. Kerry was in the hospital with toxemia, awaiting the birth of her youngest son. She was distressed of body and spirit. To bring her some cheer, a few friends snuck into her room after visiting hours. Noticing that she had not been able to wash her hair, one of them sprang into action. She got a bed pan, poured warm water into it and gently washed Kerry's matted hair. It was not pre-planned. It was not done at Kerry's request. It was a spontaneous response to a perceived need. With their warm presence, attentive concern, and some laughter Kerry's friends gave her the gift of kindness during a difficult moment in her journey.

A third example of kindness that I think of often involves a man named John Baron, who attended Saint Philip's United Methodist Church, my first pastorate. Every month, John sent a card with a short note attached to all those members of the church who were shut ins. He might simply write: "Thinking about you." "Praying for you." "Hoping you are feeling a little better these days." Or "You are loved." He asked nothing in return. When I visited the recipients of John's "Ministry of Letters," they always mentioned the card they had recently received, which was usually displayed on a table by the couch or placed on a fireplace mantel. What an impact John's warm and supportive words had on his hurting fellow travelers.

Kindness is a gift that connects us as human beings and brings hope, comfort and healing. It is also one of the easiest gifts to cultivate and share. It can be as simple as a comforting word, a reassuring presence, or an encouraging smile. So why wait? As the Quaker saying I keep on my desk enjoins: "I expect to pass through life but once. Any good, therefore, that I can do, or any kindness I can show to any fellow creature, let me do it now; let me not defer or neglect it, for I shall not pass this way again."

Practice kindness. When you see the positive effect it has on others and experience the internal fulfillment it brings, you'll quickly make it a habit.

Reflections

+ How has someone shown you kindness? How did it make you feel?

+ When was the last time you gave the gift of kindness to someone else? How did it make you feel?

+ Is there someone you find it hard to be kind to? Why?

CHAPTER 3

The Gift of Empathy

*"Empathy is about finding echoes
of another person in yourself."*
—Mohsin Hamid

*"Empathy is simply listening, holding space, withholding
judgment, emotionally connecting, and communicating
that incredibly healing message of you're not alone."*
—Brené Brown

*"I believe empathy is the most essential
quality of civilization."*
—Roger Ebert

At some point, all of us desire the presence of another person who listens, cares and understands. We want someone who knows what we are experiencing under the surface, who can feel the anxiety, fear, and sadness that we feel. We want someone to be with us who *gets us*.

There have been those times in my own life when unanticipated crises—the death of a child, a divorce, a lost job, a cancer diagnosis—have resulted in excruciating psychic pain and emotional upheaval. During those times, the empathy of others has sustained me, healed me, and given me hope.

Empathy—the ability to understand and share the wounds of another—can make a significant difference to the person who is experiencing pain, suffering, and loss. It is a life-giving gift that resides in the heart of every one of us.

Jesus is the quintessential model of empathy. He lived his life seeing and responding to those who had debilitating diseases, to those who were confused and searching for direction, to those who had made serious mistakes and unwise choices, and to those who were suffering deep loss and grief. I think of the story of Lazarus.

Jesus went to the tomb of Lazarus knowing that he would resurrect the dead man. "Our friend Lazarus has fallen asleep," he told his disciples, "but I am going there to wake him up." Yet, Jesus's awareness of what was to come did not preclude empathy. We read in the Gospel of John:

When Mary reached the place that Jesus was and saw him, she fell at his feet and said, "Lord, if you had been here my brother would not have died." When Jesus saw her weeping, and the Jews who had come along with her also weeping, he was deeply moved in spirit and troubled. "Where have you laid him," he asked. "Come and see, Lord," they replied.

Jesus wept. (John 11:32-35 NIV)

Jesus feels the pain of the mourners and shares in it, even though he knows it is only a temporary state and that soon they will be rejoicing. Jesus weeps for Mary, Martha, and the others experiencing the loss of Lazarus; and he weeps because he feels the loss himself.

I find this story especially moving because it reminds me of the humanity of Jesus and the power of tears as an expression of empathy and connection. As a minister, I have officiated hundreds of funerals and memorial services. I have heard some very moving, sensitive eulogies. On many occasions, I have felt myself welling up. Not knowing the deceased has not blocked my identification with the loss of the family. Likewise, there have been those times in my own experience when family and friends have sat and cried with me, showing understanding and bringing comfort. It is difficult to feel alone when someone is crying with us.

We can cry together because we are all so human. We can be empathetic because we are all human beings who have experienced, in one way or another, the full continuum of emotions. We have all known the joy of life, the celebration of beauty, and the love of friends. We have all been broken, rejected, bereaved, and afraid.

Yet, it is also in our nature to deny others the gift of empathy.

Too often, we get lost in our own worlds and become self-centered, particularly when our energy is consumed by our own internal conflict or external discord. Michel Quoist in his book, *Prayers*, puts words to this experience of becoming locked in ourselves, the prisoners of our own pain. "I hear nothing but my own voice. I see nothing but myself," he writes.[1]

It doesn't have to be this way, though.

I think of my daughter, Carrie, whose first child, Sydnie, was born with cancer. Although Sydnie is a healthy teenager now, her first few years were full of setbacks and she continues to deal with chronic health issues. As her daughter's primary caregiver, Carrie has faced unimaginable challenges and ridden a rollercoaster of emotions. It would have been easy for her to sink into self-pity and despair. Instead, Carrie has used her experience to further cultivate the gift of empathy.

Carl Rogers, an innovative therapist, writes: "We think we listen but rarely do we listen with real understanding, true empathy." Carrie is a person who listens with understanding and empathy. She can relate to the pain of others in a deep, authentic, and meaningful way. When Sydnie was old enough and out of the woods medically, Carrie decided to put this gift to work. She went back to school to earn a master's degree in counseling.

To give the gift of empathy, we must decenter ourselves and center others. At the same time, we must keep our *shared* humanity front and center. So many of us have a tendency to rush to blame and judgment of each other. We find it easier to focus on the faults, weaknesses, and poor choices of others than to consider what brought them to where they are or to try to see things from their vantage point. I will never forget the wisdom of my Auntie Violet who, hearing a person disparaged, said calmly, "You need to walk a mile in their shoes before criticizing them." Although we can never truly feel what another has gone through or experience their journey, we can find empathy by looking inward and reflecting upon the obstacles we ourselves have faced and missteps we have made.

We would do well to remember the admonition of Jesus: "Why, then, do you look at the speck in your brother's eye and pay no attention to the log in your own eye?" (Matt. 7:3 GNB) Empathy requires that we recognize that no human being is inherently better than another and that we all have needs and desires, histories and imperfections. When we are able to recognize our own human frailty and fallibility, we not only learn to be more tolerant, but we can also use those experiences to connect with others.

Years ago, while participating in an encounter group, I shared a dream I had in which I harmed my mother. The content of the dream startled me. Sensitive to my internal disruption, the facilitator led me through an exercise in which I explored the wounds and resentments at the root of my dream. Another woman in the group was assigned to take on the role of my mother and responded as I unpacked and relived painful events in my childhood. In the midst of my tears, the woman reached out with warmth and tenderness. She received my emotional outpouring with no judgment or qualification.

Amazingly, this psychodramatic session not only brought me a greater sense of peace within but also liberated me to give the gift of empathy to my mother. I was able to connect to my mother in shared humanity and acknowledge that she, given the difficulties of her own journey, loved me the best that she could. After the event my then-wife observed that I treated my mother differently, with more patience and kindness. The saying "See the light in each other, be the light for each other" became a transformational reality for me.

Empathy connects us across our differences around the one thing we all have in common. To be empathetic is to embrace our own humanity, accept the humanity of others, and be human *with* and *for* each other. What a wonderful gift.

Reflections

+ When did a person show you empathy? How did that experience make you feel?

+ When have you showed someone empathy? What was the circumstance generating care and support?

+ Are there certain situations or people that fail to elicit empathy from you? Why is that? Do you want to do anything about it?

CHAPTER 4

The Gift of Compassion

*"The best portion of a good man's life: His little,
nameless, unremembered acts of kindness and love."*
—WILLIAM WORDSWORTH

"Compassion is an action word with no boundaries."
—PRINCE

*"Only the development of compassion and
understanding for others can bring us the
tranquility and happiness we all seek."*
—DALAI LAMA

I am considering the gift of compassion at a difficult time in the history of our country. We have a vaccine to protect against COVID-19 and yet millions of people will not be inoculated. How do we address the rise of hospitalizations and deaths which continue to climb, mostly among the unvaccinated? We see the pain and suffering of so many seeking asylum on the Mexico/Texas border. How shall we address the whole issue of immigration? We are stunned by the violence in our cities. How do we deal with the root causes of this dilemma? We view the lines at food distribution centers where too many still lack the basic necessities of life. What can we do about this sad commentary on our society, where we have phenomenal wealth yet poverty is so prevalent?

Compassion, according to Karen Armstrong in her book, *Twelve Steps to a Compassionate Life*, means "to endure (something) with another person, to put ourselves in somebody else's shoes, to feel her pain as though it were our own and to enter generously into his point of view." It compels us, she asserts, to look into our hearts, discover what gives us pain, and then, as a result of that self-discovery, to refrain from inflicting that pain on anybody else under any circumstance. In sum, it is the Golden Rule: *Do* unto others as you would have them *do* unto you.[1] The emphasis on *do* is mine because compassion requires more of us than thinking or feeling.

Compassion is quite different from pity in this way. Pity is when we feel sorry for someone who has just lost a job, been evicted from a residence, or finds it difficult to feed their children. On the other hand, compassion is similar to empathy, which also involves seeing things from another's perspective or experiencing their emotions. What sets compassion apart, according to the University of California at Berkley's *Greater Good* magazine, is one key aspect; compassion comes with an impulse to help.[2] We give the gift of compassion when we act on that impulse.

Jesus is deeply concerned about care for others and offers a model of compassionate behavior in the Parable of the Good Samaritan. A man has been attacked by robbers and left wounded on the road. A priest and a Levite, recognized religious leaders, see the wounded man and walk on by. A Samaritan, himself a member of a marginalized community, encounters the same man. He sees the hurting person, stops, and renders assistance. He puts aside his personal agenda to attend to the needs of the other. He pours wine on the man's wounds and bandages them. He puts the man on his own donkey, takes him to an inn, gives money to the innkeeper to take care of him, and promises to pay any outstanding bill on his return journey. What an amazing story of compassion in action!

Like the Samaritan, many of us feel the burden of our brothers and sisters who are hurting from insensitivity and injustice. We understand that we are called not just to empathize but also to engage the issues that wound and scar the human spirit, to transform the systems, beliefs, and behaviors that dehumanize. We want to be not just people of words but also people of action. We want to give the gift of compassion freely, but too often we respond like the priest and the Levite; we walk by, held back by our fear, our personal comfort, or our self-interest. Worse yet, sometimes, we find it difficult to even feel compassion in the first place.

The reality is that our society operates under a paradigm that deems some human beings as "untouchables," where some people are considered unacceptable or less acceptable than others. In her book, *Caste: The Origins of Our Discontents,* Isabel Wilkerson argues that there is a caste system in the United States and compares it with that of India. "Both systems," she writes, "live on in hearts and habits, institutions and infrastructures. Both countries still live with the residue of codes that prevailed for far longer than they have not."[3] Many of us find it easier to place blame and responsibility on others than find compassion for them, even when their struggles have been shaped by these circumstances that we ourselves have created or perpetuated. It is crucial that we come to a conversation about the gift of compassion with an awareness of how we categorize people, the implicit assumptions we make about others, and how we treat them as a result.

I recently watched a film, *Come Sunday,* that tells the story of a radical change experienced by Pentecostal Bishop Carlton Pearson. Pearson was the pastor of a mega church with a diverse, growing congregation in Tulsa, Oklahoma. He was an evangelical who preached that there is only one way to God. Jesus, from his exclusive religious perspective, was the source of salvation. To be saved, a person had to consciously recognize their sinful state, confess their sins, and open their heart to receive Jesus as Lord and Savior. If a person did this, they were assured of heaven. If not, upon death, they would go to hell for all eternity.

Then, he watched a program in which children in Rwanda were dying in the hundreds of thousands from malnutrition and starvation. As he observed their anguish, he heard God's voice speak directly to him: "There is no hell! All are saved!" The theological position he had verbalized for so many years no longer made sense to him. His preaching changed; his life was transformed. He saw the face of God in every person.

When Pearson shared his position that there is no hell with his congregation, they rejected him and his message. Put off by what he understood as hypocrisy, he left the Apostolic Church. Today, he ministers at a Unitarian Church, where he no longer just preaches about compassion; instead, he lives it. By opening his arms to all people, Pearson makes real God's care for all of creation.[4]

Here's the deal. The Bible is clear that compassion is not just sensitized thinking and a saddened heart. It is not something that one has for some people and not for others. Compassion is active and inclusive, and incumbent upon those who would call themselves Christians. Micah, the prophet, asks: "What does the Lord require of you but to do justice, to love kindness, and to walk humbly with God?" (Micah 6:8 NRSV) Or, as the Message translates Micah's directive: "Do what is fair and just to your neighbor, be compassionate and loyal in your love, and don't take yourself too seriously—take God seriously." The prophet Isaiah speaks to the self-righteous religious, telling them that God is not concerned about fasting and sacrifice. What God wants is for people to show justice and care about the widow, the poor, and the marginalized. (Isaiah 58:1-10 GNB)

In a conversation, a friend of mine told me that he had only recently internalized the meaning of the Parable of the Last Judgment—that whenever and wherever a person shows kindness and compassion to the hungry, the sick, or the homeless, one is doing it unto Jesus himself. It is a message we would all do well to take to heart. Compassion compels us to give every person respect and dignity. It demands that we smash the walls that cause division and alienation.

Even our enemies, Jesus reminds us, are worthy of the gift of compassion for no one is better than another person. The rain falls on the just and unjust alike. "This is what God does," he advises, "He gives his best—the sun to warm and the rain to nourish—to everyone regardless: the good and the bad, the nice and nasty. If all you do is love the lovable, do you expect a bonus? Anybody can do that…Live out your God-created identity. Live generously and graciously toward others, the way God lives toward you." (Matthew 5:43-48 TM)

In a conversation about human fulfillment, the Dalai Lama and Archbishop Desmond Tutu emphasize that the human tendency toward compassion is instinctual. "We are hardwired to connect and care." If we go against it, the Archbishop suggests, there can be deleterious consequences for us. Compassion is absolutely essential for "it is like oxygen."[5]

Karen Armstrong, who I mentioned earlier, writes not only that compassion "is natural to human beings" but also that it is "the fulfillment of human nature, and that in calling us to set ego aside in a consistently empathetic consideration of other, it can introduce us to a dimension of existence that transcends our normal self-bound state."[6] I like the way the Archbishop talks about this. He describes each of us as a "God carrier." When we care for the other, we are being the very presence of God. In doing so, we experience a joy that nothing else can bring. This notion that compassionate care for the wellbeing of others is the source of our own happiness is at the heart of the Dalai Lama and Archbishop's dialogue.[7]

During his conversation with Archbishop Tutu, the Dalai Lama suggests that compassion is a skill that can be cultivated if we have the desire to do so. I submit that recognizing our shared humanity and understanding that we are all one family inhabiting a shared home called Earth is the greatest motivation we will ever find to want to take care of one another.

Consider our current predicament. The pandemic has put a spotlight on our connectedness as human beings and, as a result, has inspired countless acts of compassion. In the midst of this tragic public health crisis, we have seen nurses hold the hands of dying patients; neighbors come together to provide for one another's basic needs; and musicians lift our spirits by giving free concerts from their windows and balconies. We have seen the best of humanity expressed through acts of compassion.

We have also learned about the importance of extending the gift of compassion to ourselves. Parents have been frazzled working full-time jobs from home while tending to children. Healthcare workers have been driven to the depths of exhaustion and depression working around the clock, unable to stop the ravages of coronavirus. Teachers have struggled with learning new technologies and adapting to virtual environments. Most of us have witnessed or experienced unprecedented loss, whether of livelihood or lives. We are all only human and self-care is critical if we are to continue caring for others.

Give the gift of compassion to yourself and all people. This is how we make the world a more livable, loving place.

Reflections

+ How has a person given you compassion? Explain.

+ What blocks you from being compassionate to others?

+ Are you compassionate with yourself? Why or why not?

CHAPTER 5

The Gift of Helpfulness

*"Help your brother's boat across, and
your own will reach the shore."*
—HINDU PROVERB

*"Life becomes harder for us when we live for others,
but it also becomes richer and happier."*
—ALBERT SCHWEITZER

*"The human being who lives only for himself finally
reaps nothing but unhappiness. Selfishness corrodes.
Unselfishness ennobles, satisfies. Don't put off the joy
derivable from doing helpful, kindly things for others."*
—B.C. FORBES

While shopping at a grocery store, I took note of the red shirts all the associates were wearing. On the back of each shirt was this question: "Can I help you?" Immediately following the question was an affirmation: "Yes I can!" What an amazing world we would have if we lived the statement on the back of those shirts. As Albert Schweitzer wrote: "You don't live in a world all your own. Your brothers (and sisters) are here, too." It is crucial that we understand that if we are to be fulfilled human beings we must help one another.

Let's begin this conversation about the gift of helpfulness with honesty and admit that there are those moments when all of us are broken. Every one of us at one time or another needs assistance, support, or guidance.

For more than a decade, I served as Dean of Students at a university. When I talked to parents and freshman at orientation about how to approach university life, I described the many resources available to them on campus, from counseling and medical to tutorial, spiritual, and vocational help. I urged them to reach out to others and use these resources. I wanted them to know that they were not alone in this new place. Help was there. They just needed to ask for it.

There is a group exercise for partners in which one person lies on the floor and the other stands by, ready to provide help. The partner on the floor needs only reach up and the other will take their hands. Inevitably, there are those participants who cannot or choose not to reach up. To do so would be a blow to their pride, a negation of their personal power and independence. They want to appear able to meet any challenge on their own.

Too many of us think that asking for help is a sign of weakness. In actuality, it is an indicator of strength. If we are willing as human voyagers to acknowledge our own vulnerability, there are resources to assist us during the uncertain and difficult moments of the journey; so many professionals, friends, and neighbors who are willing to lend a helping hand if only we have the courage to reach out and reach up.

There are those of us who are afraid to ask for help out of fear of rejection. People will spurn me if they really know my problems, we think. Not so! Take someone who struggles with an alcohol addiction but fears being turned away or tagged as a liability. It is true that not everyone will be willing or capable of lending them support and some might even judge them. But those who are willing and capable are out there and their help can be transformational. I have had the honor of observing up-close the workings of Alcoholics Anonymous and have seen first-hand how that community steps up to care for all its members. There is someone out there to lift each of us up no matter what.

The certainty of faith is that we are not discarded because of our frailties, shortcomings, or poor choices. The Prodigal Son wastes his father's money and is in a despairing place. He comes to his senses and returns home with a confession upon his lips. "Father, I have sinned against God and against you. I am no longer fit to be called your son." His father's heart is filled with celebration. His lost son has been found. Rather than receive his son's confession, he welcomes him back into the family. (Luke 15:11-24 GNB).

Listen, we are all in this journey together. All of us make mistakes and many suffer hardships. There is no shame or deficiency in admitting that we are neither invincible nor all powerful. The fact is, we need each other. I like the Hindu proverb: "Like the body that is made up of different limbs and organs, all mortal creatures exist depending upon one another." Dependence is an inherent part of the human condition.

Jesus asks us to give the gift of helpfulness generously. He directs us to feed the hungry, clothe the naked, visit the sick and provide hospitality. (Matthew 25:31-40 TM) He does not turn away those who come to him in need. Take the story of Blind Bartimaeus, who calls out to Jesus for help. "Son of David! Have mercy on me," he cries. The crowd scolds him for disturbing the teacher. But Jesus hears him, stops, and asks that Bartimaeus be brought to him. Jesus does not complain about his boisterous plea. He does not ask, "What's wrong with you?" No. Jesus asks, "What do you want me to do for you?" In other words: "How can I help you?" The blind man, keenly aware of his immediate need, tells Jesus what he wants. "Rabbi," he answers, "I want to see again." Jesus does not respond by saying the man asks too much. He does not demand that Bartimaeus explain his loss of vision or offer him something in return for his help. He simply helps. Bartimaeus is healed. (Mark 10:46-52 TM)

Paul tells us in Galatians that each of us must ultimately carry our own load, but we are to help carry one another's burdens and, in this way, fulfill the law of Christ. (Galatians 6:2 GNB) It is incumbent upon each of us who endeavor to walk the Jesus way that we recognize our own need and seek the help necessary for healthy living because only when we accept our own humanity are we prepared to be helpers, healers, and sharers of burdens.

Many years ago, I read a book entitled *The Difficult Business of Helping.* That title sticks with me because it is so true. Helping others is not always easy. In fact, it can at times stir up very difficult questions. I remember back in the 1970s and 80s when I was working at the People's Emergency Center, a weekend shelter for homeless families, some of the people we served would ask for money to buy cigarettes and alcohol.

On another occasion, years later, my son Steven and I were taking a walk on a university campus in Philadelphia when we were asked for a handout from someone on the street. We responded that we would be glad to buy the person a meal from one of the food trucks parked nearby. "No," the man said, "I don't want that stuff." What did he want? If we gave him money, would he use it to purchase food or drugs? When faced with such requests, what is the Christian response? What is the ethical response? What is our responsibility to answer a cry for help that may ultimately bring harm? There are no easy answers to these questions.

On the one hand, providing everything that a person asks for can be enabling behavior. Too many families, for instance, protect the addict by providing basic needs and not advocating for rehabilitation. On the other hand, we need to be wary of our own cynicism and careful about a paternalistic approach to helping.

One day, my son Riley and I were at a mall when a woman approached us and asked if we had five dollars. She had run out of gas, had no money with her, and needed to get home. Having been approached so many times over the years by people requesting money I was very suspicious. I began asking questions, analyzing the legitimacy of the request. Where is your car? Where is the gas station? How come you ran out of gas? Once I was satisfied with her answers, I began to reach for my wallet only to discover that Riley was already holding out a five-dollar bill. Following the example of Jesus helping the blind man, Riley answered the woman's call for help. No questions asked. I admire that.

So many of us want to be helpers in the world. But in answering the cry for help, we often think we know better than others what they need. True helpers listen to those they want to help and treat those in need with the dignity and respect due to every person. To need help is not to be less than. Again, we will all find ourselves in need of help at some point.

The gift of helpfulness can be realized in countless ways. Sometimes it looks like a hot meal or a five-dollar bill. Sometimes it is as simple as shoveling snow for a neighbor or pulling up weeds from their garden. Helpfulness may be reading and writing notes for someone who has lost their sight or tutoring a grandchild who needs some extra help in math. It may be acting as a sounding board for someone who needs to get something off their chest, advocating against an injustice, or empowering someone else to help themselves. My brother, a marriage counselor, recently received a communication. It was a thank you note from a former patient who shared that Tom helped saved his life.

We can all make a difference in each other's lives by actively doing what we can to assist a brother or sister in need. If we are to be Christ-like people, we will readily ask "Can I help you?" and our response will always be, "Yes, I can—and I will!"

Reflections

+ How have people been helpful to you?

+ What have you done to be helpful to others?

+ What do we have to do as a nation to be helpful to people in need?

CHAPTER 6

The Gift of Presence

*"It's not your presents that matter.
It's your Presence that matters."*
—BEN WINDLE

"My presence speaks volumes before I say a word."
—MOS DEF

*"When someone is going through a storm, your silent
presence is more powerful than a million empty words."*
—ANONYMOUS

I recently had a conversation with a friend who had just returned from visiting his grieving brother. The brother had lost his wife of thirty-eight years, during which time the two had been inseparable. While at his brother's house, my friend heard his brother sobbing in the bedroom below him. With tears in his eyes my friend told me, "I didn't know what to do. I felt so bad for him." As we talked, I assured him that he had done the best thing he could. He made the effort to spend a week with his brother. His presence was a special gift.

There are many occasions when we want to do something or say something to help another person who is hurting emotionally. We want to offer uplifting words. We want to give a proven prescription for alleviating internal pain. There is, however, often nothing we can say or do to heal them. An individual must bear their own burden. What we can do is be a companion during this dark passage on their journey. Knowing that we are not alone at such times can comfort in ways that nothing else can.

As a minister, I have spent a great deal of time with individuals who are in distress, who are sick, and who are dying. So, it is not unusual for a family member or friend to ask me what to say when they visit a terminally ill person in the hospital. I often share this experience I had visiting a patient.

The man was suffering from sclerosis of the liver and was confiding in me about his fear of death. While he was talking, a nurse interrupted and chided him. "Don't talk that way," she said, "You can't think dark thoughts." This has always bothered me. It was not her place or mine to tell the man how he should deal with his own feelings. I was not there to speak or advise. I was there to lend a comforting presence and a listening ear.

So, my best advice is this: if you are visiting someone in pain, let them set the agenda. Be there to listen, to hold their hand, to say simply, "I love you and I am here for you." Your presence is a gift that means more than any platitude and is more precious than any bouquet of flowers you might bring.

I think about all the people over the past two years who have died in the hospital from COVID-19 without the presence of their loved ones by their side. What a tragedy. Thank God for the nurses who have served compassionately as surrogates. With warmth and caring, they have given the gift of their gentle presence. It has made all the difference, not only for their dying patients, but also for the family members who could not be there themselves to say goodbye.

Presence is a powerful but quiet gift. It is less about doing than it is about being. When my wife, Kerry, and I are together, we don't always need to talk or interact. Sometimes, we just sit quietly on the sofa, reading our own books in silence and enjoying the heat and light emitted from the flickering flame in the fireplace. During these times we are giving one another the mutual gift of presence.

I recently read a colleague's newsletter in which he shares a story from a man named David. David took his nine-year-old daughter to a coffee shop. Sitting at the table, the daughter made a special request of her father. "Daddy, can you not read the paper or doodle or check your e-mail today? Can we just be together?" The daughter was asking her father for the gift of presence. He gave it. That day, he put away every distraction and the two sat together, talking about ordinary things and listening to one another.

There are, of course, times when we cannot be physically present. After my first wife and I divorced and I moved out of the house, I called my children every day to check in. They have since confided in me that although my daily calls were annoying at the time, in retrospect, they cherish them. I was letting them know that I was present for them even when I couldn't be there in person. Those calls helped them through a difficult transitional moment in their young lives.

When someone chooses to be with us, they are demonstrating unequivocally that they care and we are valued. I have friends who will travel an hour to eat lunch with me because our friendship is a priority. On the other hand, I know people who are so involved in their own schedules they cannot fit others into it. They consider it wasted time to just sit and talk for nothing is being accomplished. These people need to be doing and get restless if they feel they are not accomplishing something tangible. Perhaps you are one of them. Perhaps knowing what a gift your presence can be will help you to think about productivity in a new way. Is finishing a report or running an errand any more valuable or satisfying than the impact you might have just by being with another person?

Consider the impact that Jesus had on Zaccheus when he called up to the little man in the tree, "Come on down. I want to stay with you today." That simple invitation transformed Zaccheus in terms of his thinking and acting. At the end of their time together, the unscrupulous tax collector told Jesus he would pay back those he cheated four times as much and that he would give half of his property to the poor. (Luke 19:5-8 CEV) The gift of Jesus's presence changed Zaccheus's life and made him a better human being.

There are many gifts you can give. Don't forget the powerful gift that your presence is in the life of another.

47

Reflections

+ When was the last time you were present to another human being? Who was it? How did it feel?

+ When did you appreciate the presence of a family member or friend who listened to your story? What was happening in your life at that time?

+ Who haven't you visited in some time who might benefit from your presence? What are you going to do about it?

CHAPTER 7

The Gift of Listening

*"The word 'listen' contains the same
letters as the word 'silent'."*
—ALFRED BRENDEL

"You can't fake listening. It shows."
—RAQUEL WELCH

*"Listening is about being present,
not just about being quiet."*
—KRISTA TIPPETT

When I graduated from seminary, I was assigned a church in Philadelphia. It was not a good appointment. After several months I realized that this particular congregation was too conservative for me, and I was not conservative enough for it. I wanted to grapple with social justice issues. The congregation wanted to focus on maintaining a pristine facility in which to worship. This priority was clear in the church's slogan, "The Church Beautiful." I remember there was a gang who considered the corner where the church was located their turf. They wanted to use the church gym, which had recently been refurbished. They were refused for fear they would scratch the floor. What a missed opportunity for connection!

One Sunday, I called a friend to express my frustration and disappointment with the values of the congregants. It was a very difficult moment, a test of faith, for me as a newly ordained minister. I needed to talk. But thirty seconds into our conversation, my friend shifted the conversation to his own agenda. This might seem like no big deal, but I recall it vividly all these decades later because it was such a significant moment in my own journey. I needed someone to listen, really listen, and all my friend could do was talk.

We all want to be heard. We want our story to be appreciated. When someone truly listens to us we feel validated and valued. At a funeral service for Lou Scott, a former principle of Penncrest High School, one of Lou's colleagues commented that when Lou was talking to you, there was no one else in the world. That is what real listening looks like. To give the gift of listening we must be fully present in the moment and fully attentive to the person speaking. This means decentering ourselves and tuning out everything else.

Unfortunately, in today's world, where we are inundated by information and distractions, this feels increasingly difficult to do. There are so many things constantly competing for our time and attention. We find it difficult to slow down and pay attention to anything or anyone for any substantial period, and we rarely want to. We put a premium on productivity and it comes at the price of our relationships with people.

Long ago, I read a book called *Creative Brooding* by Robert Raines. One of the sections, "Too Busy to Listen," recounts the story of a young man with a record of delinquency. He writes to tell his parents that he is going to Chicago to start some kind of new life, explaining:

Remember when I was about six or seven and I used to want you to just listen to me? I remember all the nice things you gave me for Christmas and my birthday and I was really happy with the things—about a week—at the time I got the things, but the rest of the time during the year I really didn't want presents, I just wanted all the time for you to listen to me like I was somebody who felt things too, because I remember even when I was young I felt things. But you said you were busy. . .If anybody asks you where I am, tell them I've gone looking for somebody with time because I've got a lot of things I want to talk about.[1]

The young man in the story laments his parents' priorities. In their go-go-go life, he came second. But even when we pause in the midst of the whirlwind, it doesn't mean that we are prepared to listen.

I'd venture to say that most of us have had the experience of being mentally checked out when someone is talking to us. I know I have. One particular occasion that comes to mind was when I was serving as Dean of Students. I was facing an urgent project deadline that could not be completed without certain information from one of my staff. As I was waiting at the main desk for the statistical data I needed, a student came up and began talking to me. After several minutes he waved his hands in front of my eyes as if to say, "Are you there?" Awakening from my mental meandering, I realized that I was not listening to the student at all.

What does it say about our values when we can't be bothered to stop and hear another's story? What could possibly be more important than listening to what is on a child's mind and heart? What data could be more pressing to a Dean of Students than the concerns of a student?

I think about this lesson from the Gospel of Luke. Jesus comes to the house of Martha and Mary. While Martha is in the kitchen, frantically getting dinner together, Mary chooses to sit in the living room listening to their visitor's teachings. "Lord, doesn't it seem unfair to you that my sister just sits here while I do all the work," Martha asks Jesus. "My dear Martha," he replies, "you are worried and upset over all these details! There is only one thing worth being concerned about. Mary has discovered it..." (Luke 10: 38-42 NLT) Jesus appreciates the listening ear over the hustle and bustle of meal preparation.

Listening is a crucial dimension of communication and vital to the establishment of healthy relationships. Without it, there can be no "meeting of meaning," no constructive resolution of conflict, no building of trust. But it is a human capacity that few of us know how to use or put in the effort to develop. In fact, too often we engage in conversation not because we truly care about what another person thinks or feels but because making conversation is a social expectation.

As minister at Lima United Methodist Church, I tried an experiment. When a member of the church asked me how I was I doing I would say something challenging. For instance, I told one person I was doing terrible. The person responded by saying "That's great!" and then continued on his way down the hall. The words went in his ears but he did not process them. He was asking how I was as a nicety; the answer did not matter.

"Remember this, my dear friends," we are exhorted in the book of James, "Everyone must be quick to listen, but slow to speak. . ." (James 1:19 GNB) How far this is from the behavior most of us practice in our daily living! The fact is, rather than listening to understand and empathize, most of us listen only to respond. We don't like prolonged silences in our conversations. When there is a gap, we leap to fill it. We feel that we must always have advice ready in response to another, even when they are not looking for it. Rather than ruminating on what another person is saying as they are saying it, we are formulating what we will say next. Perhaps worst of all, we come to our exchanges with others closed. We already know that we are right and the other person is wrong. We have our statements prepared before the conversation even begins. As the pioneering Gestalt therapist Fritz Perls observed, "It's very rare for people to talk and listen. Very few listen without speaking. Most can speak without listening."

Theodor Reik, a psychoanalyst, encourages us to listen with the third ear. That is, we are to be aware of our own internal feelings and to practice listening to the deeper levels of meaning expressed by the other. We are also reminded that communication is not only verbal. We must listen with ears *and* eyes, taking in the whole individual. So much can be conveyed in a facial expression, a voice intonation, or a body posture. The reality is, if we are attentive, a person's non-verbal signals can tell us what their words do not. Imagine a person who responds to the question "How are you?" with "I've never had a bad day." If you are really listening, you will take note of the glassy eyes, slumping shoulders, and softness of speech that tell a different story.

Jesus was not only a teacher but also a consummate listener. He heard the cries for help even in the midst of a busy day. He saw needs expressed verbally and nonverbally. He was not just present physically but was also keenly attentive. Jesus didn't hear words without acknowledging them. He didn't respond in ways that ignored the substance of what had been expressed. Never did he casually dismiss someone's deep concern. Jesus never replied to a struggling person with the words "Okay, I heard you" and then, turning to his disciples, said glibly, "Let's go to lunch." Absolutely not. Jesus listened to understand and when he responded it was always with intention.

In Jesus, we find a model of what the Zen Master Thich Nhat Hanh refers to as "deep listening." He explains the concept in an interview with Oprah:

Deep listening is the kind of listening that can help relieve the suffering of another person. You can call it compassionate listening. You listen with only one purpose: to help him or her to empty his heart. Even if he says things that are full of wrong perceptions, full of bitterness, you are still capable of continuing to listen with compassion. Because you know that listening like that, you give that person a chance to suffer less. If you want to help him to correct his perception, you wait for another time. For now, you don't interrupt. You don't argue. If you do, he loses his chance. You just listen with compassion and help him to suffer less. One hour like that can bring transformation and healing.[2]

In our country today, people seem more divided than ever. Our tendency to *speak at* each other while never *listening to* each other only exacerbates the problem. Certainly, it offers no healing bridges. Imagine how different things might be if each of us committed to practicing the art of deep listening.

One last thought on listening. Like most of our human gifts, this is one that we cannot give fully to others until we have given it to ourselves. Yet it seems that we are just as bad at this aspect of communication when it is internal as we are in the context of external conversation. Consider, when was the last time you set aside time to do nothing but sit with your thoughts? Have you ever?

Mindfulness and meditation are two techniques that can help us tap into what we are really thinking or feeling and engage in meaningful interior dialogue. When we embrace silence and pay attention to our inner soundings, we can find healing, comfort, and enlightenment within. There is a Native American proverb that says it best: "Listen to the wind, it talks. Listen to the silence, it speaks. Listen to your heart, it knows."

Today, make it a priority to listen more and talk less.

Reflections

+ Are you a good listener? How might you be an even better listener?

+ Recall an instance when someone gave you the gift of listening. How did it feel? To whom do you want to give the gift of listening today? Why?

CHAPTER 8

The Gift of Touch

"Human touch is a premium thing."
—HARJEET KHANDUJA

*"Too often we underestimate the power of touch,
a smile, a kind word, a listening ear, an honest
compliment, or the smallest act of caring, all of
which have the potential to turn a life around."*
—LEO BUSCAGLIA

*"The human touch is that little snippet of physical affection
that brings a bit of comfort, support and kindness.
It doesn't take much from the one who gives it, but it
can make a huge difference in the one who receives it."*
—MYE ROBARTS

Though no less important than our other capacities, touch is gift that we must approach with heightened sensibility and awareness. We have to be careful about who we touch and how we do so. We must recognize that not everyone appreciates the gift of touch and acknowledge that toxic touch—touch that is unsolicited or inappropriate—can cause harm, ranging from mild discomfort to major trauma.

With the outbreak of coronavirus, we have also learned to be cautious about tactile contact for reasons of physical health. We no longer shake hands but bump elbows. We no longer give spontaneous hugs but virtual hugs. Instead of sitting by a loved one and holding their hand as they pass away, we say our goodbyes through screens and over phones. At the same time, our present predicament creates anxiety, loneliness, and fractured relationships—the very things that touch can soothe and heal. By denying us touch, COVID-19 has awakened in us a newfound appreciation of its power. I would urge you, in your family constellation, where parties have been vaccinated and masks appropriately worn, to resume the sharing of hugs. They are needed more than ever.

Max Muller suggests that a flower cannot blossom without sunshine and that people cannot live without love. I affirm the truth of this statement and also affirm that touch, as an expression of love, is essential to the development and wholeness of the human being. As human beings we all need touch. When it is appropriate, welcomed, and safe, it is a magnificent gift.

Studies have confirmed that touch is an essential ingredient of survival. For babies, a lack of touch can lead to developmental impairment, or even death. For adults, touch may not be necessary for life, but research suggests a correlation between a lack of touch and negative health outcomes. In contrast, certain kinds of touch have been shown to contribute to our physical, psychological, and emotional wellbeing. Touch can reduce blood pressure, pain, and inflammation by inhibiting cortisol, the stress hormone. It can also trigger the release of oxytocin, dopamine and serotonin, the so called "feel good" chemicals. As a result, it promotes trust and security.[1] Touch, as one psychologist writes in her blog, "is more than just biological. It's part of the human language, nurturing emotional needs, validating affection, and quenching fears."[2]

Jesus knew the power of touch to bring healing, clarity, and hope. I have always found a story from the Gospel of Mark particularly inspiring in this respect. At Bethsaida in Galilee, Jesus is asked to heal a blind man. He takes the man by the hand and leads him out of the village. He puts spit in the man's eyes, lays hands on him, and asks him, "Do you see anything?" Looking up the man responds, "I see men. They look like walking trees." So, Jesus lays hands on his eyes again. The man looks hard and realizes that he has recovered perfect sight, seeing everything in bright, twenty-twenty focus. (Mark 8:22-26 TM). Is it any wonder that so many clamored for Jesus's touch?

After curing Simon's mother-in-law of a high fever in Capernaum, Jesus is confronted by a crowd of others suffering from various ailments. Listen to this action taken by the man from Nazareth: "One by one he placed his hands on them and healed them." (Luke 4:40 TM) Jesus turned no one away. The gift of touch was given to all who were in need.

In my own life, I have known how it feels to live in the absence of touch. Growing up, my twin brother, Tom, and I never had a warm or reassuring hug from my mom nor would she accept one from us. Her own upbringing with an alcoholic father had stunted the development of this capacity within her. She stiffened when human contact was offered.

When my brother and I were just one and a half years old, we lost our father. My mom, wanting the best for us, enrolled us at Girard College, a residential school for orphans and fatherless children located in Philadelphia. As you might expect, comforting hugs and emotional support were not in abundant supply at Girard. For a child thirsty for affection, even the smallest gesture was profound. My brother's bed was located by the doorway leading out of the dormitory. He later shared with me that one of the governesses, Ms. Stacks, after turning off the lights, would often tousle his hair on her way out. It was a simple gift of touch that was transformational; Tom felt cared for.

Having rarely received physical affection in my childhood, it always surprised me when I was a student at Dickinson College to see one of the older professors walking across campus holding hands with his wife. Although I found this public display of tenderness strange, it made a deep impression on me. I yearned to know what it felt like to experience such an easy and unselfconscious expression of love.

Over the years, I have witnessed how a gentle arm around the shoulder can sustain and bring comfort in times of loss and grief. I have seen how one person can give assurance to another with a pat on the back. I have watched how pain and suffering can be made bearable when one grasps the hand of a nurse or loved one. To touch is to say "You are loved." "You are supported." "You are not alone."

Although it frankly took me many years, I am glad to say that I eventually learned to give and receive the gift of touch freely. I know the feeling of warmth that comes from holding hands with my wife and the joy of receiving a giant bear hug from my youngest granddaughter on the days when she's not feeling shy. In fact, over the years, I have become a hugger. I fully subscribe to the teaching of family therapist Virginia Satir who wrote: "We need 4 hugs a day for survival. We need 8 hugs a day for maintenance. We need 12 hugs a day for growth."

I remember a sermon I preached at Riddle Village, a retirement community, in which I emphasized the value and importance of a hug. A senior commented at the conclusion of the worship service that she had not been hugged for over two years since the death of her husband. I asked her if she wanted a hug. She said she would. I gave her a hug. She cried. There are few things that can communicate care, connection, empathy and understanding like a welcomed hug.

When given thoughtfully, carefully, and with consent, the gift of touch can say what a million words cannot.

Reflections Reflections

✦ Think of a time when someone gave you a hug that really made a difference in your journey. How did it feel?

✦ Are you comfortable giving and receiving touch? Why or why not?

✦ How do you ensure that someone else is open to receiving the gift of touch before you share it?

The Gift of Acceptance

"It is who I is."
—Tom Peterson

"If I am not for myself, who will be for me? If I am not for others, who am I for? And if not now, when."
—Talmud

"It is enough that I am of value to somebody today!"
—Hugh Prather

I used to be a member of Planet Fitness. On numerous occasions as I was leaving the facility, I would stop to read their mission statement on the wall. The gym, it says, provides a unique environment where everyone can feel comfortable. It is a judgment free zone where diversity is appreciated. The closing sentence of the statement pronounces acceptance: "We need you, because face it, our planet wouldn't be the same without you. You belong!"

Jesus would have approved.

The understanding that every individual is special and loved by God is central to the gospel. God's gift of grace extends to all people; it is not exclusionary. We are all worthy. Jesus demonstrated by example. He did not heal a blind beggar because he professed a certain creed. He healed a Roman officer's servant as readily as he raised a widow's son. Where there was need, Jesus responded. He did not treat people differently depending on their color, ethnicity, belief, gender, or sexual orientation.

I have always been moved by the encounter Jesus had at the home of Simon, the Pharisee. It is a classic story. Jesus is invited to dinner by a prominent member of the community. In the town there is a woman who has lived a sinful life. She hears that Jesus is eating at the Pharisee's house so she goes to see him. She brings a jar full of perfume. In a spontaneous act of love and appreciation, she wets Jesus's feet with her tears and dries them with her hair. She kisses them and pours the expensive perfume on them. Simon, full of self-righteousness, responds: "If this man really were a prophet he would know who this woman is who is touching him; he would know what kind of sinful life she lives!" No, Jesus informs him. You have it all wrong. Her love is that much greater because she has been forgiven so much. (Luke 7:36-50 GNB) What a special account of acceptance. It makes me want to be more appreciative of others and encourages me to be a better human being.

In the spirit of transparency, I will admit that I have found it a struggle to accept all people on an equal basis, to acknowledge that all human beings are special. I find it especially difficult to deal with those who are narcissistic, arrogant, and myopic. My experience tells me that I am not unique. Whether we are driven by our personalities, backgrounds, cultural stereotypes, or ignorance and fear, we humans often deem others unacceptable and treat them accordingly.

If we are to live Gospel values, those followed and taught by Jesus, we must consciously and intentionally push aside these barriers that disconnect and alienate us from each other. Acceptance must be an essential component of our behavior. I hear these words reverberating through my brain: Accept him as he is! Accept her as she is! Accept them as they are! Everyone is a child of God!

We would do well to remember that we, too, are children of God. I am and you are. It is not only that we have difficulty accepting others. Too many of us find it challenging to accept ourselves. During years spent as a minister, counselor, and dean, I have had countless conversations with people, young and old, who have trouble seeing their own worth. With tears in their eyes, these hurting individuals have confided in me that they are not pretty enough, intelligent enough, or personable enough. They have expressed that they feel inadequate, unaccomplished, and unlovable. They are plagued with self-doubt and punish themselves with self-deprecation.

Sadly, such toxic internal dialogues frequently arise, or are inflamed, when the individual has experienced a lack of acceptance by others or holds themselves to impossible standards set by parents, partners, or society at large. Writer and retired surgeon, Bernie S. Siegel suggests "the fundamental problem most patients have is an inability to love themselves, having been unloved by others during crucial parts of their lives." A vicious cycle is created. We do not feel accepted; we do not accept ourselves; we do not accept others.

The flip side of this is the boost that acceptance from another can give to our self-esteem. Having lost my father as a baby, I had no parental relationship model, and going to an all-male school, I had no opportunity for significant interaction with the opposite sex. I spent most of my young adulthood doubting my looks and personality and feeling anxious about how I came across to my female peers. I carried that anxiety with me not only through school but through two marriages as an adult!

It wasn't until I found my soulmate, my wife Kerry, that some of my old wounds and feelings of inadequacy have begun to heal. You see, Kerry loves me unconditionally. With her, I know that I do not have to prove my worth. I am accepted as I am. I am loved because I am. What a gift her acceptance is! It is a gift that I return.

Accepting each other as we are, by the way, does not mean that either of us is perfect or that we don't have habits that the other finds annoying. I, for instance, drive Kerry crazy when I ask too many questions or sit chewing ice in front of the TV. Acceptance means that we are loved *with* all our idiosyncrasies not despite them.

It is a wonderful thing to have someone who loves you "to the moon and back" and accepts you for you like Kerry and I do. But, ultimately, self-acceptance has to come from within. If we base our self-acceptance on the way another person perceives us or the status they lend us, what happens when that person is no longer around or their perception of us changes? Louis L'Amour offers a healthy perspective in the novel *Comstock Lode*. Mr. Hesketh, perturbed that Margrita Redway is not interested in marrying him, suggests that she is missing out on being "somebody." Margrita replies: "But I am somebody, Mr. Hesketh. I am *me*. I like being me. And I need nobody to make me somebody."

It might take meditation and reflection, it might even take professional help, but we would all do well to cultivate the kind of unqualified self-acceptance that Margrita expresses. Once we are able to accept ourselves, we will be fully liberated to give the gift of acceptance to others.

I am special because I am, and you are special because you are. When we are able to affirm that for ourselves and each other, we can turn pain into peace and divisions into connections. The gift of acceptance is truly transformative.

Reflections

- Do you feel good about yourself? Why or why not?

- Who do you find it difficult accepting? Why?

- What will you do to become a more accepting person?

CHAPTER 10

The Gift of Affirmation

*"I love watching how my positive statements
dissolve negativity in others."*
—Charlene M. Proctor

*"Celebrate you! You are worth celebrating. You are
worth everything. You are unique. In the whole world,
there is only one you… No one can take your place."*
—Clyde Reid

"I can live for two months on a good compliment."
—Mark Twain

In *Have a Little Faith,* we read an account of Henry, the minister of an inner-city Detroit church. Henry is leading a worship experience. His congregants are poor. They are lacking many advantages. But he wants his church family to know that everyone among them has value. He shouts, "I am somebody." The people respond, "I am somebody!" He reinforces the affirmation: "I am somebody." The people respond once again: "I am somebody!" Would that we could always feel this truth with such certainty. I am somebody.

If, as the theologian Paul Tillich, writes "the courage to be is the courage to accept oneself, in spite of being unacceptable," then I submit the joy of being is the joy of affirming oneself as a person of infinite worth, made in the image of God and endowed with the potential to change the world.

Affirmations are positive comments that comfort, compliments that encourage. They indicate more than acceptance. They are proclamations of the light within us and the grace that envelopes us. Affirmations are reminders that each of us is special and blessed from the day we are born to the day we die. Our value as humans is not earned. It simply is.

My son, Chris, works for a company that provides tools and services to help entrepreneurs and small businesses. He has told me many times how important affirmation is in his approach to relationship building. Even within a business context, Chris recognizes that his clients and associates are still human! He lets them know that he values them not just as professional contacts, but also as people. I'm not surprised that Chris is quite successful in his work.

There are so many ways we can affirm one another—easy ways that cost us nothing and have incredible impact. I will always remember, for instance, a resident of a retirement community who told me in all seriousness that she was an angel. I asked her how she came to this marvelous realization. "Well," she told me, "every time I get on the elevator, I smile at the people who are passengers with me. Some of them look pretty glum. So often, when I smile, they smile back. I help to make their day better." A simple, sincere smile can be a way to let another human being know that they are seen, that their very existence is a cause for rejoicing.

Kind words, shared sincerely, can also be a special gift of affirmation. Rather than focusing on what someone does, let them know that you appreciate them for who they are. For example, you might say to a child, "You are special. I am so blessed to be your parent." To a friend you might say, "I cherish having you in my life." To a partner, you might say "I love you for all that you are" or "You are truly the best thing that has ever happened to me."

Every time I read about Janet in Henry Nouwen's book *Life of the Beloved,* I am moved. Janet is a member of the L'Arche-Daybreak Community in Toronto, Canada, a residential home for the physically and mentally challenged. She asks Henri, the priest, for a blessing. He casually makes the sign of the cross on her forehead. She tells him that she wants a real blessing.

That evening at a prayer service Henri acknowledges her request. With her head on Henri's chest, she receives the gift of affirmation she craves:

Janet, I want you to know that you are God's Beloved Daughter. You are precious in God's eyes. Your beautiful smile, your kindness to the people in your house and all the good things you do show us what a beautiful human being you are. I know you feel a little low these days and that there is some sadness in your heart, but I want you to remember who you are: a very special person, deeply loved by God and all the people who are here with you.[1]

When I first read this passage, I cried. It touched me at a deep level. I suppose because I was able to identify so closely with Janet's need.

When I was growing up, my home church told me that I was a sinner who had to win God's approval. So, I tried in every way possible to be the obedient Christian. But nothing I did made me feel secure in my relationship with the divine. I was left with the constant, nagging question: Was I good enough? Unfortunately, this approach was not limited to the church of my youth. Many church communities continue to dispense toxic messages suggesting that people must somehow atone for being human and work to earn salvation.

In my case, the idea that one's value is acquired rather than intrinsic was reinforced at home. My mother, a human being who carried deep psychic and emotional wounds, could not affirm me through words or affection. I remember how I felt when I brought home a report card with all A's and maybe one B. "Mom, what do you think," I inquired. Her response still gnaws at me. "You know I like all A's." What a difference it would have made if she simply said, "I know you did your best. I'm proud of you."

No matter how good my grades, no matter how many awards I claimed or trophies I won, it never seemed to be enough for my mother. I will never forget one of the phrases she used to repeat over and over: "Good, better, best, never let it rest, until your good is better and your better is best." All I wanted was to be loved and valued for who I was, not because of how close I came to some unreachable bar of perfection. I always struggled, and still do on occasion, with the belief that my value correlates with my external achievements.

The damage we do to one another can be significant. It is easy to be affirming, but it is just as easy to make someone feel insignificant, unseen, or inadequate, whether we intend to or not.

Another one of my mother's favorite maxims that stills lodges in my brain is "Sticks and stones may break my bones, but names will never hurt me." I could not disagree with this statement more. As surely as a compliment or caring word can uplift us, a thoughtless comment or unkind barb can decimate us, shaping our sense of self for years to come. For this reason, the Buddha instructs his students to think before speaking, cautioning them to refrain from gossip, slander, and malice of any kind. Every time we open our mouths to speak, we make a choice. As the book of Proverbs cautions: "What you say can preserve life or destroy it, so you must accept the consequences of your words." (Proverbs 18:20-21 GNB)

Scripture offers us so many examples of those who fail to affirm the divine in their fellow human beings. There is Simon the Pharisee who dismisses the woman with the bad reputation. There are the disciples who castigate the parents who bring forth their children to be blessed by Jesus. There are the people who complain that Jesus has chosen to spend the day with the tax collector Zaccheus. In each case, Jesus recognizes the inherent value of the individual and offers affirmation through word and deed.

Jesus, Buddha, and Muhammed, too, challenge us to be people who build others up, not tear them down. We are to let others know they are special not because of what they do but because of who they are. When we give the gift of affirmation, we recognize the divine potential of our fellow humans and realize the divine potential within ourselves.

Lisa Ernst, a meditation teacher and visual artist, writes this simple prayer: "May all beings be seen. May all beings be heard. May all beings be cared for with compassion and love."[2] I add to this: May all beings be affirmed.

Every day, take a moment to remember: you are somebody and so is everybody else.

Reflections

Reflections

+ What affirmations have others given you that have made a difference in your journey?

+ Do you readily give genuine, authentic affirmations to others? Whom do you recognize and how do you compliment them?

+ When was the last time you saw someone smile because of special words you shared with them?

CHAPTER 11

The Gift of Time

*"It's really clear that the most precious
resource we all have is time."*
—Steve Jobs

"Never leave 'til tomorrow what you can do today."
—Benjamin Franklin

"Time is what we want most, but what we use worst."
—William Penn

My Timex watch has been on my wrist for years. During waking hours, it has methodically let me know how long I have been on the stationary bike, how long the steak has been on the grill, and how long I have to get ready before leaving the house for an appointment. At night, as darkness has enveloped the world, I have lit up its face to see how much time I have to return to a slumbering state. Today my watch lost its charge. It died! So, will I.

As I get older, not only do I have more aches and pains, but I have also become acutely aware of my mortality. I find myself reading the obituaries in the newspaper, looking to see if anyone I know has died and studying the ages at which people have passed on. As I do so, I think about my priorities. I want to be more intentional about the way I use the time I have left.

None of us wants to reach the end of our days and regret how we lived. Yet I have talked with many adults who have expressed regret over not spending more time with their children. Some have admitted that they have been fixated on work to the detriment of their relationships. Others have lamented a lack of self-care over the years. So many of us put off the things that truly matter, thinking that there will be time for them later, only to wake up one day and realize that later is now and now is too late.

The truth is, none of us know how many days we have remaining to us on this earth. Having worked on a university campus for many years, I am well aware of the tendency of the young to think they are indomitable and will live forever. Yet, there are many adults who miscalculate the duration of their life as well. I think of one woman whose mother lived to be ninety-six; her aunt, too, lived well into her nineties. She assumed, based on family longevity that she would also live to a ripe old age. When this lovely lady contracted a serious and ultimately fatal lung disease in her late seventies, she was stunned. Life did not proceed as she had envisioned it. It might be cliché, but we really would do well to cherish each day as though it were our last.

Likewise, we cannot predict the time left to those special people in our lives. I have officiated at hundreds of funeral and memorial services. Too many times, I have heard mourners say things like "I intended to visit them, I just didn't make the time." It leads me to wonder about the all the baskets of flowers sent in memory of the deceased. What kind of relationship did the sender have with the person who died? Did they "make the time" for this friend or loved one when they could? Why do so many of us wait until a person is gone to express our love and appreciation?

The thing about time is that we have no control over it. We cannot stop it or slow it down. The only thing we can control is how we spend the days we are given. For my part, being a relational person, I am choosing to spend as much time as possible with the people I love—enjoying their company, being present for them, and hopefully creating memories of warmth and affection that will live on when my journey is completed. Flowers for the living, right?

When I think about the gift of time, I once again think of Jesus. Jesus was a living answer to the question "If not now, when?" Even though he was on a mission with a limited window to realize his goal, Jesus always had time for people. He was never too busy to respond to the needs of others—to minister to the sick, feed the hungry, care for the hurting, or give hope to the hopeless.

Choosing to walk the way of Jesus compels us to give the gift of time in service to our human family. Many years ago, I read a poem in the publication *Guideposts* that speaks to this call. I cannot quote it line for line, but I believe that it went something like this:

Today my hands are strong so let me help you. Tomorrow they may be weak or old or sick and you will have to lighten my load. But today my hands are strong so let me help you. For why do we exist, if we cannot walk each other's path or feel each other's sorrow? Neighbor, today my hands are strong so let me help you.

What more sacred use of our gift of time could there be than to give it to our fellow brothers and sisters who are hungry, lonely, depressed, frightened, vulnerable or marginalized?

My daughter, Jennifer, does not consider herself a religious person, but she understands the connection that exists among all humans and is committed to trying to make the world a more beautiful, compassionate, and just place for everyone. She spends countless hours writing postcards, calling representatives, and attending rallies. She advocates for artists, immigrants, and women. She works to empower voters of color and stop voter suppression. Several years ago, she left a good job in Manhattan and moved back home with her mom to make an independent film about the positive difference affirming healthcare can make in the lives of transgender youth. Although I selfishly wish she would spend more time with her father, I am proud of the choice she has made to expend so much of her time and energy on behalf of the people and causes she champions. (I am also truly grateful for the time she has set aside in her busy schedule to edit this book.) Frankly, I am not sure how she finds enough time in the day to do everything she does.

Giving the gift of time can be transformational for the recipient and giver alike. To the one who on the receiving end, the gift of time can come with a message of care, affirmation, compassion and love. For the one giving the gift, it can bring an unmatched sense of purpose, meaning, and fulfillment.

But what I hope for my daughter and for all those who give the gift of time so generously to others is that they remember to give the gift of time to themselves as well. We all need time to rest, refresh, and revitalize. Sitting on a porch enjoying the quietness and gentle breeze, leisurely sunbathing, watching a sunset colored in pastels, comfortably meditating, listening to one's favorite music, reading a book, or exercising—such activities enable wellness.

Paul Tillich, the theologian, talks about the idea of "Holy Waste." He does not mean by this that we should throw away sacred time. What he means is that we should take the time to care for self and appreciate the wonder and miracle of creation.[1] Thich Nhat Hanh in his book, *The Art of Living*, challenges the reader to do the same when he asks: "Do you have time to enjoy the glorious sunrise? Do you have time to enjoy the music of the falling rain, the birds singing in the trees, or the gentle sound of the rising tide?"[2]

The fact is, time is a priceless and precious gift, "a portion of your life that you will never get back," as the saying goes. It is up to each of us to choose how we want to use it. There are no excuses. We make time for what we feel is important.

To give of our time is to give of ourselves. Use your gift of time wisely.

Reflections

+ Have you ever consciously tracked how you spend your time? What have you discovered? If you have never engaged in such a task, why not?

+ What do you do for others?

+ What would you like to do that you are not doing? What are you going to do about it?

CHAPTER 12

The Gift of Patience

*"Patience is not the ability to wait, but the ability
to keep a good attitude while waiting."*
—ANONYMOUS

"He that has no patience has nothing at all."
—ITALIAN PROVERB

"A handful of patience is worth a bushel of brains."
—DUTCH PROVERB

As important as I know patience to be, I must confess that it is not the most developed of my human gifts. Some years ago, while on my way to a speaking engagement in the Northeast section of Philadelphia, I got caught in a traffic jam around 30th Street Station. I knew this meant I would be late for my event. I hate to be late, and the more I sat there in the car going nowhere, the angrier and more agitated I became. My impatience was getting the best of me.

Why, I asked myself, was I getting so upset? There was no way to change the situation. I could not leave my car in the road and walk to the event. I could not get a helicopter to escape the traffic problem. The only way out was to flow with the situation at hand. I would get to my appointment when I got there. I would apologize and hope that people understood—which they did.

This was one of many opportunities I have had to exercise the advice offered in the book of Proverbs: "Hot tempers start fights: a calm cool spirit keeps the peace." (Proverbs 15:18 TM). Also this: "If you stay calm, you are wise, but if you have a hot temper, you only show how stupid you are." (Proverbs 14:29 GNB). It was one of my more successful efforts. Other opportunities have not gone as well.

I will never forget a little league baseball dinner that my son Steven and I attended some four decades ago. As a parent, I sat with the coaches at the head table. The players sat at tables of their own. It did not take long for the shenanigans to start. First, the boys dumped their canned fruit appetizers in the middle of one of the tables. I was irritated, but the coaches seemed oblivious to this conduct. So, I tried to ignore it as well. I was managing with some effort…until the spaghetti and meatballs were served.

My aggravation grew as I watched some of the boys empty their plates on the heads of others. Why didn't the coaches stop the nonsense? Then I saw my son join in the food flinging melee. I could not restrain myself. I ran to his table and began a loud reprimand. He made some disrespectful remark. I lifted him up and told him we were leaving. Some parents quickly came to his aide and settled me down.

I knew that I had handled the incident poorly. I was not calm and I was not wise. My impatience got the better of me and my temper triumphed over equanimity. I made my son the scapegoat for the misbehavior of many, and I made a fool of myself. Only within the last several years has my fifty-year-old son assured me that I have been forgiven for my actions.

The writers of the New Testament challenge us to be individuals who live with calm and a gentle presence. Paul writes that love is patient and kind. One of my favorite passages of scripture is found in Colossians: "You are the people of God; he loved you and chose you for his own. So then, you must clothe yourselves with compassion, kindness, humility, gentleness, and patience." (Colossians 3:12 GNB). I think of the question raised in Galatians: "But what happens when we live God's way?" And the answer:

He brings gifts into our lives, much the same way that fruit appears in an orchard—things like affection for others, exuberance about life, serenity. We develop a willingness to stick with things, a sense of compassion in the heart, and a conviction that a basic holiness permeates things and people. We find ourselves involved in loyal commitments, not needing to force our way in life, able to marshal and direct our energies wisely. (Galatians 5:22-23 TM)

Patience is at the center of our efforts to be people living a life of excellence grounded in Gospel values.

I am inspired by the enduring patience of Jesus. He did not become flustered by the crowds of sick people wanting his attention. He was not bothered by the little children interrupting his teachings. He stayed calm and collected when confronted by naysayers and unbelievers. (Luke 20:18, 19-26 TM).

However, I also take comfort in knowing that none of us humans is perfectly patient. Not even Jesus who, exasperated by the self-righteousness of the Pharisees, responded with these harsh words:

You are like tombs that have been whitewashed. On the outside they are beautiful, but inside they are full of bones and filth. That's what you are like. Outside you look good, but inside you are evil and only pretend to be good. (Matthew 23:27-28 CEV)

Learning to be patient is difficult. It requires awareness, motivation, intention, and action. Dealing with the relentless crying of a child, waiting to hear about a new job possibility, attempting to reconcile a conflict between hostile parties, dealing with forgetful older people—all require energy, mindfulness, and internal dialogue. We all have to work at being patient.

Although I have developed my patience a great deal since that long-ago little league dinner, I still find my patience tested regularly. I get frustrated with myself, for instance, when I fail to accomplish an established goal. I yell at cars that pass me only to cut in front of many other cars. "Don't let him in" has been my mantra. When an associate at the grocery store chats incessantly while slowly packing the bags of the customer ahead in line, I get annoyed. I tap my fingers and check my watch during long meetings where too many people have too much to say. My capacity for patience is one that I am continuously trying to strengthen through practice.

Patience is one of the capacities resting dormant in our hearts until we decide to make it a vital part of our living. We can do it if we exert the necessary effort. While reading the obituaries in this morning's paper—I do that as I have gotten older—I read about a woman who died at ninety-nine years of age. It was said of her that she was loved by everyone who had the privilege of being in her company. Now here are words that really spoke to me: "She was kind, caring, and a sweet gentle person who many have said had a 'sparkle in her eyes' throughout her entire life with a gentle presence and calming affect that fell over those she loved like a blanket." Clearly, this woman had cultivated and shared the gift of patience.

May we all develop such inner tranquility, made manifest in a life lived with a smile and gentle spirit.

▨ **_Reflections_** ▨▨▨▨▨▨▨▨▨▨ Reflections ▨

✦ Are you a patient person? Why? Why not?

✦ With whom or with what do you have to cultivate more patience? How will you do this?

✦ Are you patient with yourself? What enables you to have this attitude?

CHAPTER 13

The Gift of Friendship

*"A real friend is one who walks in
when the rest of the world walks out."*
—WALTER WINCHELL

*"There is nothing on this earth more
to be prized than true friendship."*
—THOMAS AQUINAS

"Of all possessions a friend is the most precious."
—HERODOTUS

In the Old Testament, we read the story of Naomi, who lost her husband and sons while living in Moab. Hearing that there is a good harvest in Judah, Naomi decides to go there, accompanied by her two daughters-in-law. As they journey on their way, Naomi encourages the younger women to go back home to their own mothers. She expresses the hope they will each find a new husband and begin a new life.

Orpah kisses her mother-in-law goodbye but Ruth holds onto her and says these moving and memorable words: "Don't force me to leave you; don't make me go home. Where you go, I go; and where you live, I'll live. Your people are my people, your God is my god; where you die, I'll die, and that's where I'll be buried, so help me God—not even death itself is going to come between us!" (Ruth 1:6-7, 16-17 TM)

Would that everyone could experience such a friendship!

Over the years, I have posed this question to a number of people: What is a friend? I have received myriad responses. All agree that a friend is someone you can trust and rely on. Many bring up qualities such as acceptance, understanding, openness, forgiveness, and laughter. Confidentiality is mentioned as key. One of my students described a situation in which her best friend shared with another person something that was not for public consumption. She was crushed and, as a result, found it difficult to trust people in general. Ultimately, the answers I have heard might best be summed up in the words of author and philosopher Elbert Hubbard, who wrote that a friend is someone "who knows about you and loves you just the same."

My own understanding of the gift of friendship is this:

In the eyes of a friend we can see who we are—valued and loved. Friends challenge us and want the best for us. They do not always agree with our thinking or behavior and correct us accordingly. A friend can be trusted with our secrets, joyful or painful though they might be. The sharing between friends is mutual. A true friend readily opens up about their weaknesses, as well as their strengths, and gives you a non-judgmental space to do the same.

A friend is a person with whom you enjoy spending time. They are someone you can laugh with and cry with. Someone who is there to lift you up in celebration and support you through your brokenness and emotional distress. Friends are attentive, caring, and understanding. They are always there for you with a hug, a smile, a tear, or a word of encouragement—and vice versa. Such a relationship is restorative, it promotes equilibrium and helps us fulfill our human potential.

As humans, we need the gift of friendship to thrive. We forget at times that Jesus was a human being who experienced the same continuum of emotions that we all experience. He, too, needed friends. He selected twelve men to walk the dusty roads of Galilee with him. From that group the chose Peter, James, and John to be his closest companions. They experienced with him the mystery of the transfiguration as well as the despair in the Garden of Gethsemane.

In my own life, I have been so fortunate to have wonderful friends. I am blessed to be married to my best friend, Kerry, whom I have mentioned so many times in this book. Two of my closest friends have been my siblings—my sister, Dot, and twin brother, Tom. Dot, now deceased, used to be my road companion. Whenever I was driving, I would connect with her on my mobile phone via Bluetooth (hands free, of course!). We would chat about how our day was going and discuss pertinent issues involving our families. I still talk with Tom twice a week. It has become a ritual, Mondays and

Fridays. We catch-up, share remembrances, and frequently discuss our opposite political views. Our calls frequently go on for an hour or more. Both Dot and Tom have given me the gifts of listening and love along with their friendship.

One of my closest confidantes over the past thirty years has been a friend from my days at Drexel University. Tom and I have shared many laughter-filled lunches together; we have tried to crush one another on the tennis and racquetball court with enthusiasm; and we have engaged in numerous, serious conversations about the state of the world and the current political crisis in our country.

Another long-time friend who made a significant difference in my journey was Dan, an ex-priest who filled my life with much humor and deep theological commentary. Dan recently died, but he will remain with me in so many ways. Gordon is a friend I met when I officiated at his wedding some twenty-five years ago. I smile every time I think of his mother-in-law who came into the church on his wedding day and said to me in a stentorian voice, "Oh, you must be Gordon's son." I still call him dad to remind him of his age.

When I think of my friends, a Nigerian proverb comes to mind: "Hold a true friend with both your hands." I do not take my friends for granted. I know that their friendship is a gift to be prized and cherished.

Friendships are divine connections with our fellow human travelers. They are not, however, automatic. They cannot be purchased or coerced. We must make them a priority and build them through investments of time and self. When we do, they are one of the greatest sources of meaning and fulfillment to be found, bringing warmth, joy, wisdom, and comfort to our journeys.

What a gift to have someone you can call friend. What a gift it is to be a friend to another human being.

Reflections

+ Do you have a close friend? What makes that person so important to you?

+ Do you make friendship a priority in your journey? Why or why not?

+ How do you let your friends know they are special to you?

CHAPTER 14

The Gift of Vulnerability

"What makes you vulnerable makes you beautiful."
—Brené Brown

"To share your weakness is to make yourself vulnerable;
to make yourself vulnerable is to show your strength."
—Criss Jami

"We all need somebody to talk to. It would be good if we
talked. . . not just pitter-patter, but real talk. We shouldn't
be so afraid, because most people like this contact; that you
show you are vulnerable makes them free to be vulnerable."
—Liv Ullmann

I approach this chapter about the gift of vulnerability with some hesitation. Why? Because if I am to convey the importance of vulnerability I must be willing to be open and authentic in my sharing.

It is not always easy to let someone else into our interior space—our thoughts and feelings. Often, we choose carefully with whom we will disclose these depths of our personhood. This, however, I know to be true: there is reciprocity in being transparent. When I am open to others, they are more likely to be open with me. It is then, when walls are taken down, that connectedness and community can emerge and flourish.

As I have noted before, my youth was spent largely at a residential school in Philadelphia, called Girard College. It was an institution for orphans and fatherless boys, which my twin brother and I were, having lost our father as babies. Girard provided an excellent academic and vocational experience but did little to meet the need for affection. After all, a governess or housemaster could not provide emotional support to thirty or so boys for whom they were responsible, and to be frank, emotional openness was not exactly in vogue during that particular period in our history.

As you can probably imagine, as a child sent to live in an orphanage, I experienced my fair share of emotional turmoil in the form of uncertainty, fear, and insecurity. I recall moments at Girard when I was walking the long road to my residence hall feeling lonely and quite sad. I would have liked a hug. Did I tell anyone? No. I knew that no one would really care to hear about it.

At Girard, I learned very early to keep my feelings to myself, and in fact, became very good at it. To the external world I was a well-behaved little gentleman. People often commented on how polite I was and how proud my mother should be. They did not know about any pain or brokenness I experienced on the inside.

In his book, *A Better Man: A (Mostly Serious) Letter to My Son,* the writer and comedian Michael Ian Black reflects that "The first two rules many boys learn—"no sissy stuff" and "suck it up"—put boys in an emotional pen." He relates that he grew up in this pen.[1] I did, too. Girard indoctrinated me in the belief that the suppression of emotions was a sign of strength.

I remember singing with gusto the words of Girard's Alma Matter at seven years of age: "Harvard loves her crimson banner, Yale her blue divine; In our pennant, bold and stirring, steel and garnet shine. Brown is busy making scholars, so is valiant Penn; Our Girard, our Alma Matter, she is making men." "Men," as defined by Girard, did not cry, they were always in control, and they did not ask for help. "Self-care" was not a thing.

The time I spent at home with my mother did nothing to counteract these lessons. As I have expressed at other points in this book, my mother was not a person who was able to be open with her feelings or affections. Her father was an alcoholic and she bore the wounds of that relationship her entire journey. Between home and Girard, my emotional IQ was stunted. As Black writes, "You may get through the moment, the day, the week. Eventually though, the blood stops flowing altogether, and something in you falls away."[2]

It was not until my early twenties, when I discovered the human potential movement, that I was finally freed to feel authentically and express my emotions. I learned and experienced the truth that most, if not all, human beings are broken at times and that it is okay to admit feelings of emptiness and inadequacy. I came to the realization that being "strong" was a tourniquet blocking the real me.

For five days, I became part of a beautiful, supportive, affirming, liberating community of my human brothers and sisters. I got to know people better in a short period of time than I did in my own family. I was able to be myself without pretense and was accepted for who I was.

My tendency to keep up my guard did not disappear overnight. There was another occasion while I was enrolled in a course in Clinical Pastoral Education at a reputable hospital when one of my colleagues called me out on it in a group encounter. "No one," he said, "can be as cool as you are." He was right. The comment sliced through my defenses and, suddenly, tears that I had bottled up for years gushed forth like a geyser. It was a cathartic experience that prompted an inner calm I had not felt in a long time.

Like all of our human capacities, vulnerability will lie dormant until awakened and nourished.

The idea that vulnerability is something to be avoided is one that is unfortunately pervasive in our society. I remember when I was active in ministry a conversation I had with a young man who was considering marriage. The subject of feelings came up and the young man informed me that he never cried and had trouble expressing tenderness. I asked why. To him, these were signs of weakness. I recommended some therapy to help him unpack these beliefs and start cultivating his vulnerability so that he could give that gift to his wife-to-be.

I wish that I had been able to share with him at that time a passage from Alex Trebek's book, *The Answer Is*. In his struggle with pancreatic cancer, Trebek came to a new understanding of the relationship between toughness and vulnerability. He writes:

> *I used to think not crying meant you were tough. Now I think crying means you're tough. It means you're strong enough to be honest and vulnerable. It means you're not pretending. And not pretending, being willing to let your guard down and show people how you truly feel and admit that you're a wuss, is one of the toughest things a person can do. Sharing your feelings with others brings people closer together. It demonstrates an interest in developing under-standing...It demonstrates a caring. Because you have to figure there are some people out there who are going through the same stuff.*[3]

I have, through the reading of the gospel accounts, found Jesus of Nazareth to be extremely open and expressive. He cries with Mary, Martha and others mourning the death of Lazarus. He shares his pain with his friends in the Garden of Gethsemane, telling them, "The sorrow in my heart is so great that it almost crushes me." (Mark 14:34. GNB). "In great anguish" on the Mount of Olives, "he prayed even more fervently; his sweat was like drops of blood falling to the ground." (Luke 22:44 GNB). Nailed to the cross, Jesus experiences loneliness and doubt. "My God, my God," he utters, "why did you abandon me?" (Mark 15:34 GNB) It is in his most vulnerable moments that Jesus, the human being, is most believable to me.

It seems to me that Stephen Russell, the late Taoist teacher and practitioner, was correct when he wrote: "Vulnerability is the only authentic state. Being open means being open for wounding, but also for pleasure. Being open to the wounds of life means also being open to the bounty and beauty." When we open ourselves up and let another person into our internal world, we promote connection. By letting another see my scars and brokenness, I am showing them my humanity and inviting them to reciprocate. It is then, when we are present with each other as feeling people engaged in the common human struggle that healing and transformation become possible. We become, in the powerful words of Henri Nouwen, wounded healers.

Give the gift of vulnerability. There is no greater show of strength.

Reflections Reflections

+ Are you able to be vulnerable? With whom?

+ What blocks you from being open and transparent with others?

+ Have you experienced the healing power of shared tears?

CHAPTER 15

The Gift of Forgiveness

"To err is human, to forgive, divine."
—Alexander Pope

*"Forgiveness is not an occasional act,
it is a constant attitude."*
—Martin Luther King, Jr.

*"People have to forgive. We don't have to like them, we
don't have be friends with them, we don't have to send
them hearts in text messages, but we do have to forgive
them, to overlook, to forget. Because if we don't we are
tying rocks to our feet, too much for our wings to carry!"*
—C. Joy Bell

I like to sing the hymn *Amazing Grace*. It speaks to me of the centrality of forgiveness and acceptance in the Gospel proclamation. Being human and making many mistakes in judgment and behavior, intentional and unintentional, I have celebrated and continue to celebrate the gift of grace. To know that I am received and valued by the heart of the universe is both liberating and transformational.

Jesus teaches forgiveness as an essential component of religious life. Reflecting on the importance of charity, prayer and fasting, Jesus tells his students: "If you forgive others the wrongs they have done to you, your Father in heaven will also forgive you. But if you do not forgive others, then your Father will not forgive the wrongs you have done." (Matthew 6:14-15 GNB) "How many times should a person forgive," inquires Peter, "seven times?" No, says the teacher, seventy times seven. Just as God's forgiveness is without limit, so, too, are we as Christian people to be generous in the giving of this gift.

To offer forgiveness is to acknowledge not only our capacity to be God-like but also our imperfect humanity. A passage of scripture that touches me deeply is found in the Gospel of John. A woman caught in the act of adultery is dragged before Jesus. A spokesperson suggests that she be stoned to death per the code of Moses. Jesus writes in the dirt and then stands up. His words penetrate the cloud of coldness, anger, and indifference that hangs around those ready to inflict punishment on the hurting, frightened and broken woman. "The sinless one among you," he said, "go first: Throw the stone." (John 8:8 Message) One by one, the men leave, until Jesus is left alone with the weeping woman. Tenderly, he forgives her, then sends her on her way, with the admonition not to sin again.

Forgiveness involves pardoning self and others for wrongful deeds and offenses. It does not always involve forgetting. It may involve reconciliation, but not necessarily. What it *does* entail is a letting go of resentment, anger, and a desire for retaliation. Why? Because these are emotions that cause harm to our psyches, produce internal pain, and stunt our growth. Only in forgiveness can we escape this self-imposed cell of distress and despair in order to focus on the task of nurturing our human capacities to their fullest. Forgiveness is as much, if not more, about our own wellbeing as it is about another's.

I know from experience the burden we carry when we withhold forgiveness. I had a good friend who betrayed me. The hurt lingered and weighed on me for years. I tried to negotiate a time when we could engage directly and bring closure to the situation, but he was not emotionally prepared to have that conversation. He died of a massive coronary before we were able to reconcile. I regret that to this day. I am glad to be able to say, however, that I was eventually able to find forgiveness for him on my own. My load has been lighter ever since.

We are to forgive but it is not always easy. It takes awareness, intention, and motivation to work through the internal entanglements and intense feelings that hold us back from forgiving. Sometimes therapy can help in this process—and it is a process. What we must understand about forgiveness is that it does not heal everything all at once.

I have a friend who while living with a significant other got involved with another woman. His partner eventually found out about the affair. He asked for the gift of forgiveness and she gave it. They stayed together, got married, and now have two children. However, whatever issues in my friend's psyche or in the dynamic of their relationship that led to his immature and hurtful indiscretion did not go away automatically when they reconciled. Nor did the trust that was broken between them did not magically mend when forgiveness was offered. The couple has had to use their other gifts—gifts like presence, empathy, and vulnerability—to attend to their weaknesses, heal their wounds, and strengthen their connection.

In Alcoholics Anonymous, there is a step dedicated to making amends. This involves the person going to those that they have harmed through their addiction, taking responsibility for their behavior, and demonstrating through actions, not just words, how they have changed. In making amends, the person in recovery presents the person they have hurt with an opportunity to heal, whether or not they are willing or able to accept it. For the recovering person, the goal is not to clear one's conscious but to help them get out from under the shame of their addicted behavior, freeing them to move towards a healthier life, fulfilling their potential to be of service to others.[1]

If we are to live whole lives, we must be open to receive the gift of grace and acceptance that is the promise of Jesus. Sometimes, however, the hardest person to forgive is oneself. Let us remember that as human beings, we all have our shortcomings. We all transgress. We will all know the weight of guilt, regret, embarrassment, and shame on our shoulders at some point during our journey. Acknowledging this can free us not only to ask for and receive forgiveness, but also, to give it, as we do unto others, to ourselves.

As we forgive, we are the very presence of Jesus. Amazing grace, how awesome it is.

Reflections

+ Have you received the gift of forgiveness? How did it make you feel?

+ Who do you find it difficult to forgive? What are you going to do about it?

+ Who have you forgiven? What enabled you to bestow the gift of forgiveness?

CHAPTER 16

The Gift of Gratitude

*"At times our own light goes out and is rekindled
by a spark from another person. Each of us
has cause to think with deep gratitude of those
who have lighted the flame within us."*
—ALBERT SCHWEITZER

*"I thank You God for this most amazing day;
for the leaping greenly spirits of trees and a blue
true dream of sky; and for everything which
is natural which is infinite which is yes."*
—E.E. CUMMINGS

*"If the only prayer you said was thank
you, that would be enough."*
—MEISTER ECKHART

I have preached many times about the ten lepers who were healed by Jesus on his way to Jerusalem. Ten men with leprosy stand at a distance shouting, "Jesus, Master, have pity on us." Jesus hears them and tells them to show themselves to the priest who has the final say as to whether or not they can return to society. As they go, they are healed. Nine of the men, we assume, return joyfully to their families. One man, a Samaritan, returns to Jesus, bows down at his feet and thanks him. "Weren't ten men healed," Jesus asks, "Where are the other nine?"

I wonder how many of us would be the thankful one.

So many of us fail to appreciate the gifts we have been given. The more we have, the more it seems we take our riches for granted. I had a real sensitizing experience a few years ago when I traveled on a mission trip to Haiti. We spent our time there building 10' x 12' houses. For many of us, this was the size of the sheds, stuffed full of unused belongings, that we kept in our backyards. But for the families who would live in these houses, it was enough. Our storage sheds were their needed shelters. They were grateful, and I was reminded in the starkest of terms how much I have to be grateful for. The grateful person is the aware individual who notices and appreciates the blessings of life, however big or small, simple or abundant.

When I was young, my mother always directed me to express thanks when I was given a gift. One Christmas I received a metal picnic basket full of cookies from a well-intentioned aunt. I was not impressed. I'm sure I wondered why it couldn't have been a toy, a comic book, or a baseball mitt. My mother, however, was firm in her insistence that I write a thank you note. So, I did.

As a child, I resented having to write a thank you note

for a gift I didn't feel particularly thankful for. As an adult, I appreciate the fact that my mother instilled in me the importance of giving thanks. The fact is, no matter the gift, we can be thankful for the thought, care, or generosity behind it. Today, no one needs to compel me to write a thank you note. I gladly write them of my own volition. I always try very hard to express gratitude to all of the people who through their skills, services, and human gifts bring blessings to my life every day.

What a gift it is to recognize our giftedness and what a gift we give to others when we thank them for the small and generous acts of kindness, service, patience, and understanding that they give us as a matter of course. There are so many ways to show our gratitude. We can leave the restaurant server an extra big tip or offer the landscaper a tall glass of iced tea on a hot day. We can give the nurse who has managed to take our blood painlessly a thumbs up or tell the teacher who spent extra time with us after class what a difference it made.

I was visiting an elderly person in a rehab center not too long ago when a young woman entered the room with a pitcher of cold water. "Is that for me, princess," the senior asked, "Well, thank you. Thank you so very much!" That young person left the room with a smile on her face and warmth in her heart. What a positive effect a little recognition and a word of thanks can have.

Two particular occasions from my time as a minister come to mind when I think about the power of showing gratitude.

At Lima United Methodist Church, some parishioners formed a group called the "Love Bugs." Their mission was to affirm others. One morning when going to my office I found a flower arrangement in front of the door with a note: "Thank you for all you do." My spirit soared.

More recently, I retired from a small church in Valley Forge after eight years of ministry. After my final service, a member of the church came up to me and began to say some kind words. In the midst of his speech, he began crying. My heart connected with his and the tears flowed freely. There was this beautiful moment of human closeness. His tears were a gift to me expressing his sincere appreciation for my contribution to this special church community. No words, no token of thanks could have meant more.

Gratitude lets others know that we see them, that we have received the gifts—material and immaterial—they have shared, and that we value their contributions to our lives and to the world. The gift of gratitude is not just about words. It is about the spirit in which we live and the way that we treat others. Gratefulness is a matter of words, attitudes, *and* actions. I think about all the first responders who have risked their lives and worn themselves out caring for the sick and dying during the COVID-19 pandemic. It was wonderful to see how in some cities, like New York, whole neighborhoods came to their windows to bang pots and pans to communicate their thanks. Our caregivers and health providers deserved it! They also deserve for us to do everything within our power to stop the virus so that they can take a break and care for themselves. Wearing a mask, social distancing, getting a vaccination and booster shot—these are also ways that we can show thanks.

The reality is, there are times when we will not feel grateful. The past two years have been especially challenging for the world at large and for so many of us as individuals. Bad things have happened. Good people have died. Our spirits are battered and weary. During these and other difficult moments, I encourage us to remember that life itself, with all its ups and downs, is a precious gift for which to be grateful. I often repeat the words of the psalmist: "This is the day the Lord has made. Let us rejoice and be glad in it."

The person of faith, nurturing and seeking to express their innate human capacities, lives with gratitude every day not just on special occasions. We would do well to go to bed each night and wake up each morning with a "thank you" on our lips. Ralph Waldo Emerson practiced just such gratitude. "When I first open my eyes upon the morning meadows and look out upon the beautiful world," he wrote, "I thank God that I am alive."

I remember an occasion when I was walking across a college campus with a friend, conversing about business matters. He startled me by shouting midsentence—"Jim, look at that magnificent tree!" In front of us stood a flowering magnolia tree with large pink blossoms. Had he not awakened my senses to the gift of nature before me, I would have missed a beautiful sight.

Leo Buscaglia, a writer I have turned to many times for wisdom over the years, asks this question: "Why do some people always see beautiful skies and grass and lovely flowers and incredible human beings, while others are hard-pressed to find anything or any place that is beautiful?" The answer, I believe, lies in gratitude. We see beauty in the world when our eyes are open to it, when we live life in awareness of the gifts all around us.

There was a member of my church who had a reoccurrence of breast cancer and was dying. She asked that her bed be put in the living room next to a window she could look out and see the beautiful flowers in her garden and the varied birds eating at the feeder. She wanted to be aware and thankful until her last breath. She showed me what it means not just to live with gratitude but how to die with it.

To live and die with gratitude is to follow in the way of Jesus. Despite the suffering that he saw all around him, despite the suffering that he knew he would eventually experience himself, Jesus lived his life with an attitude of thanksgiving for he found wonder and goodness wherever he went and had faith that whatever was needed God would provide.

In the book of Matthew, we read the story of Jesus feeding the five thousand. As evening fell, the disciples urge Jesus to send away the crowds so they might go and buy themselves food. No, Jesus, replies. Let them stay and give them something to eat. The disciples point out that they have only a handful of loaves of bread and two fish. We know what happened after that:

"Bring them here to me," Jesus said. And he directed the people to sit down on the grass. Taking the five loaves and the two fish and looking up to heaven, he gave thanks and broke the loaves. Then he gave them to the disciples, and the disciples gave them to the people. [20] They all ate and were satisfied… (Matthew 14:13-21 NIV)

Jesus gave thanks and broke the loaves to feed the people. Jesus gave thanks and raised Lazarus from the dead. Jesus gave thanks and called the little children unto him.

My sister gave me a Precious Moments figurine, which has a prominent place on a shelf in my home. It is a little boy wearing an elf's cap. He is painting a tree in bright colors. The caption on the figurine is a call to action: "Color your world with thanksgiving."

There is so much to be thankful for. Why not take a few moments and create a list of thanksgiving. Don't analyze but just record what comes to mind. Here are some things for which I am grateful:

+ The functioning of an amazing body.

+ The twinkle in a caring eye.

+ The flow of Christmas bubble lights.

+ The warm smile of a familiar face.

+ The peace of a restful moment.

+ The connection experienced holding my wife's hand.

+ The wagging tail of an affectionate dog.

- A magnolia tree resplendent in pink.

- A soothing shower with fragrant soap.

- A deep conversation with a long-time friend.

- A dancing child on an Ocean City beach.

- The quiet breath of life.

- A yellow rose with open petals.

- The awe-inspiring beauty of a majestic sunset.

When we give the gift of gratitude, we are in a sense "paying it forward." Our gratitude generates positivity in the world; in showing our appreciation, we lift others up and they are encouraged to do the same.

Be thankful! Recognize your riches. Celebrate your life.

Reflections

- Are you a thankful person? How do you show it?

- What are you most thankful for? Why?

- Have you ever received a memorable thank you? What was it? How did it make you feel?

The Gift of Generosity

*"True generosity is an offering; given freely and out of
pure love. No strings attached. No expectations."*
—Suze Orman

*"What we have done for ourselves alone dies
with us; what we have done for others and
the world remains and is immortal."*
—Albert Pike

*"You give little when you give of your possessions.
It is when you give of yourself that you truly give."*
—Kahlil Gibran

When I think about the gift of generosity, my son Steven comes to mind. Steven and I had just completed a father and son camping trip to Choco Canyon in New Mexico. On the last day of our special adventure we stayed at a Fairmount Hotel in Santa Fe (an experience which reinforced my preference for hotel living over pup tents). When one of the hotel housekeepers came into our room to make up the beds, my son engaged him in conversation.

Steven mentioned that we were going to have dinner in the upscale hotel dining room. The housekeeper said he had never eaten there commenting that "it sure smelled good." "You've never been there?" queried Steven. "Don't all the hotel staff have an opportunity to taste the cuisine?" Nope, this gentleman said, he had never had the privilege. My son was noticeably bothered by this reality. He found out the housekeeper's name from the front desk and comped him $250 so he could share a meal with a friend at the restaurant. He even asked me whether or not I thought that was a sufficient amount. I was moved by his generosity.

The generous individual is one who spontaneously, without analyzing, chooses to share personal resources with another. They do not give to gain anything in return. They don't even expect a thank you. Years back, I attended a recognition dinner for individuals who had given over a thousand dollars to Drexel University. In conversation with a fundraiser, I discovered there were some people who did not want their name on a donor's list. They *chose* anonymity.

True generosity is not motivated by a desire to earn accolades or prove that we are "good" people. No. True generosity has nothing to do with the giver and everything to do with the recipient. It is often an act of appreciation or compassion. Sometimes it is a pure expression of humanity. In my son's case, giving was a natural outgrowth of a deep-seated belief that all humans are of equal value and deserve not only to have their needs met but also to experience the finer things in life. Steven was disturbed by a system of hierarchy that would deny the staff who keep the business running the pleasure afforded to the guests they serve. He couldn't change the situation for everyone, but he could at least ensure this one person the experience of a good meal.

We live in a society in which it is easy to be seduced by materialistic concerns; too many of us are fixated on our own accumulation of wealth and things. We think about giving to others in terms of what it will take away from us. We justify our reluctance to share the riches we have by convincing ourselves that we are deserving while others are not. We have worked harder or done more for our communities. We have prayed more or lived "better" lives.

I think of the story of the greedy farmer told by Jesus. A rich man produces a terrific crop, much too great for his small barns to handle. "What can I do," he asks himself. A solution comes to him: He will build bigger barns! "Then I'll gather in all my grain and goods, and I'll say to myself, Self you've done well! You've got it made and can now retire. Take it easy and have the time of your life." It is a response rooted in self-centeredness. He does not think about how he can share his abundance with the poor or his neighbors who may be struggling. The story ends in dramatic fashion. He dies that very night. (Luke 12:13-21 GNB)

It is worth asking ourselves why we are stockpiling material goods and what we are saving up so much wealth for. One Thanksgiving, my family returned home to find that the parsonage where we lived had been robbed. I lost many objects that were not only expensive but also held sentimental meaning. Before I could get too upset, however, the words of Jesus thundered into my consciousness: "Do not store up riches for yourselves on earth, where moths and rust destroy, and robbers break in and steal. Instead, store up riches for yourselves in heaven . . . For your heart will always be where your riches are." (Matthew 6:19-21 GNB).

For close to a decade, I was the minister of a church in Valley Forge. It was a small church with fewer than eighty members. It was already supporting a ministry in Haiti but decided to share more of its resources with the community. Over forty thousand dollars was taken from the trustee accounts to help organizations responding to essential human needs. Most of those on the Administrative Board felt it was more important, more Jesus-like, to respond to the immediate needs of struggling people than keep the money in reserve for future emergencies. It was truly the Christian thing to do.

While a campus minister I had a conversation with a woman who wanted to live the Jesus way but was conflicted. She was completing her studies to be a lawyer. Her husband, if I remember correctly, was in medical school. With tears in her eyes, she confided that they planned to move to the suburbs to escape the poverty and plight of the city. They were going to be financially secure and wanted to enjoy the nice things their financial status would afford. With her, I shared the words of Luke: "Much is required from the person to whom much is given; much more is required from the person to whom much more is given." (Luke 12:48 GNB)

Some may experience the inverse of this woman's situation. They will say, I barely have enough resources for myself and my own family. How could I possibly give the gift of generosity to others? To them, I offer the model of Jesus, the son of a carpenter, who had no worldly riches but lived with boundless generosity. I also offer the wisdom of the Dalai Lama:

Giving material goods is one form of generosity; but one can extend an attitude of generosity into all of one's behavior. Being kind, attentive, and honest in dealing with others, offering praise where it is due, giving comfort and advice where they are needed, and simply sharing one's time with someone—all these are forms of generosity, and they do not require any particular level of material wealth.[1]

I could not write a chapter on the gift of generosity without talking about one of the most generous people I have ever known—Charles K. Hay. A former associate superintendent of the Philadelphia school system, at one point in his professional career Mr. Hay served as principal of the summer school at Girard College, the institution where I lived for most of my childhood and all of my teenage years.

Whether because they saw potential in us or for some other reason, Mr. Hay and his wife Ruth, a physical education teacher, unofficially adopted my twin brother, Tom, and me. Mr. and Mrs. Hay would have us at their home in South Philadelphia for dinner and send us back to school with a shopping bag full of mystery gifts. We were always surprised with the contents of the bag—pens, watches, ties, shirts, socks, cookies, candy, and more. The Hays bought me my first typewriter and my first suit.

When we had graduated Girard and moved on to Dickinson College, the Hays would pick up my mother and bring her to visit Tom and me for Parents' Weekend. She really loved those trips. They would always stop at a rest area off the Northeast extension of the turnpike where my Mom would order her favorite breakfast—blueberry pancakes.

Upon retirement, Mr. and Mrs. Hay moved to a senior living facility. Every month, I would try to make a point of having lunch with Mr. Hay, who was both a mentor and the closest thing I ever had to a father. We would eat at his favorite emporium, a delicatessen in a shopping center. At the end of the meal he would slide something towards me covered by his hand. As he not so surreptitiously passed me the $50 bill, he would always comment, "No strings attached."

Towards the end of his life, despite failing eyesight, Mr. Hay would send me notes from the Vesper Service he faithfully attended each Sunday. Frankly, most of the notes were illegible, but I was touched by his continuous effort to help me in my ministry.

The gift of generosity that the Hays, and Mr. Hay in particular, gave me touched my life profoundly and shaped the person that I am today. From them, I learned firsthand the power of generosity to change lives, bringing love and hope to those in need. They will be in my heart until my journey is completed.

To be truly generous is to understand that we are fulfilled as human beings not by what we get but, rather, by how we give. Give with no strings attached!

Reflections

+ How often do you give the gift of generosity? Could you be more generous? Do you want to be?

+ Describe a time when a person was generous to you. How did it make you feel?

+ Have you ever experienced greediness? What did it feel like? How did you counteract that impulse?

CHAPTER 18

The Gift of Legacy

*"Do all the good you can, by all the means you can, in all
the ways you can, in all the places you can, at all the times
you can, to all the people you can, as long as ever you can."*
—JOHN WESLEY

*"I want to be thoroughly used up when I die, for the
harder I work the more I live. I rejoice in life for its
own sake. Life is no brief candle to me. It is a sort
of splendid torch which I have got a hold of for the
moment, and I want to make it burn as brightly as
possible before handing it on to future generations."*
—GEORGE BERNARD SHAW

*"If I can stop one heart from breaking,
I shall not live in vain."*
—EMILY DICKINSON

Some months ago, I gathered with others at Mt. Jacob Cemetery in Glenolden, PA, to remember and celebrate the life of a beloved member of the family. Nelson was sixty-two years old and had passed away unexpectedly.

My daughter—and his niece—Jennifer, wrote his obituary, which appeared in *The Delaware County Daily Times*. I offer an excerpt here:

Superhero expert, comic book collector, cigar aficionado, friend to dogs, and a lover of Asian cuisine, classic rock, and karaoke, Nelson was a man of many interests and opinions. He was an avid reader, who watched the news regularly, was always thirsty for knowledge, committed himself to self-growth, and was astoundingly punctual. Nelson was born with cerebral palsy, which bent his body but never bowed his spirit. His zest for life was contagious, his honesty unparalleled, and his loyalty to those he loved unbreakable.

The tribute went on, ending with this passage:

Nelson was the listening ear, the watcher on the walls, the tie that bound. He will be remembered and missed not only by his family but also by countless friends, neighbors, and pets whose lives were made richer and better for having him in them. Nelson's light in the world was bright and it will remain so as he returns to his place among the stars.

We will all die. That's a fact. Whether we intend to or not, we leave behind a legacy. Nelson was a person who made a difference and left behind a powerful legacy. What about you? What will your legacy be? How will you be remembered?

More than once in the pages of this book, I have noted the hundreds of funerals at which I have officiated during the course of my fifty-five-year-long ministry. What I have not said is that whenever there is the opportunity, I will meet with the family of the deceased individual to go over the details of the funeral service. I will also ask the family to share with me what lessons they learned from the loved one who has passed. It is an exercise that frequently evokes tears, and often laughter, too.

The United Methodist minister James W. Moore engages in a similar process, which he writes about in his book, *At the End of the Day*. When Moore speaks to families, he asks them to reminisce about their loved one, to think back over the scope of the person's life, and to lift up and say aloud that person's top qualities or attributes. "Kindness," "Family," "Caregiver," " and Sense of Humor" are some of the words and phrases he notes hearing often.[2]

Although it may sound morose, as I get older I think about what this conversation will sound like when my life is the topic of discussion. What will people say about me when I'm gone? What words and phrases will come to mind? Which memories will evoke tears? Which laughter? What lessons will I have taught those I loved? What impact will I have had on the world?

"My deeds must be my life," Stephen Girard, the founder of Girard College, wrote. "When I am dead, my actions must speak for me." Again, we cannot refuse or avoid a legacy. The best we can do, I submit, is live a life of intentional action. We can touch the world with our innate capacities of kindness, generosity, empathy, and love or we can contribute to the toxicity which darkens our culture and, I would suggest, the universe. We can leave behind a legacy of a constructive existence or a destructive one. The choice is ours.

At the beginning of this book, I set out the Christian framework for thinking about human gifts. I would like to return, in this final chapter, to a focus on what it means to leave behind a legacy after Jesus's own. I think most of us who call ourselves Christians would like to be able to say, as Paul did, "I have fought the good fight. I have finished the course. I have kept the faith." I think most of us would like to know in the end that we have fulfilled the words of parable: "Well done, thou good and faithful servant." With this is mind, I ask you to consider the following questions.

First, will those who survive you be able to say that you had a reverence for life? We are told in Genesis that God created life and it is good. Did you drink deeply of the stream? Were you attuned to the beauty around you? Did you acknowledge your connectedness to everyone and everything? How often did you miss the budding rose or the shooting star for lack of awareness? How often did you fail to taste your food or appreciate the warmth of the sun? The gift of life is so precious. Did you receive it, unwrap it, and live it with gratitude?

Second, will people be able to say that you were truly a person of faith? Did you doubt the presence of God during tough times, or did you trust that God never abandons us, that God is right there in the midst of our sorrows, as well as our joys. Karl Barth, the theologian was once asked to summarize his theological position. He simply said: "Jesus loves me, this I know for the Bible tells me so." Did you live your life with this certainty of God's unconditional love?

Third, will you be remembered as a person who lived a life of love? Did you understand the message at the heart of the Gospel? Jesus lifts up the example of the Good Samaritan who attends to the needs of his fellow traveler. He washes the feet of his disciples and instructs them to do the same for others. Did you give the gifts of kindness, generosity, and compassion? When you are gone from the earth, will others be able to say of you that you were Christ-like?

Many years ago, I read a story in Keith Miller's book, *A Second Touch*. A busy business executive makes the decision that he is going to try to be a Christian. Rushing to catch a train, he accidentally bumps into a boy who is carrying a jigsaw puzzle. The pieces of the puzzle end up scattered on the platform. The man bends over and helps the boy pick up the pieces, sighing as his train pulls away. The boy, realizing that his helper has missed the train, watches him closely. After the task is accomplished and the puzzle is back in the box, the boy asks the man, "Mister, are you Jesus?" In that moment, the man understands that he was.[3]

My Christian journeyer, how will you use your gift of legacy?

Reflections

+ What are your life priorities?

+ What gives your life meaning?

+ How do you want to be remembered after you leave planet earth?

Conclusion

We are all endowed, from birth, with the capacities discussed in the pages of this book—love, kindness, empathy, compassion, helpfulness, presence, listening, touch, acceptance, affirmation, time, patience, friendship, vulnerability, forgiveness, gratitude, generosity, and legacy. These are human gifts that can be nurtured, developed, and shared with others.

We can all be gift givers if we choose to be.

As Christians, we are called on to see ourselves in all of our brothers and sisters and, recognizing our connection as a human family, to give our gifts fully, generously, and freely to one another. In this way, we make real the love at the center of Jesus's teaching and living.

As gift givers we are preachers. We give sermons every day through our actions, as we strive to live our expressed values. It was said of the early Christians, "See how they love each other." We are to be lights to the world in our treatment of our fellow travelers and our investment in social change.

As gift givers we are teachers. Through our example, we help others find meaning and joy in their journey. We are to educate our children, and all those searching for direction, about the values and priorities of Jesus. Our lessons are to demonstrate that relationships are more important than things and that wholeness is to be found in human connection.

As gift givers we are the wounded healers. Having experienced our own brokenness, illness, grief, and loneliness, we care for others in their suffering. As humans who have been there, we are to find empathy and offer acceptance and grace.

As gift givers we are the presence of God. We celebrate the fulfillment of our potential as sources of hope, light, and love. We are to throw open our hearts, minds, and arms and proclaim that Christ is alive through us.

Let today be a new beginning for each of us as we awaken to the sacredness of life and seek to be what God has called us to be. We are to be gift givers.

Notes

Biblical Resources

Holy Bible—Contemporary English Version (CEV). American Bible Society, 1991.

Good News Bible (GNB). American Bible Society, 1976.

The New Interpreter's Study Bible (NIV). Abington Press, 2003.

New Living Translation (NLT). Tyndale, 1996.

New Revised Standard Version of the Bible (NRSV). National Council of the Churches of Christ, 1989.

The Message (TM). NavPress, 2002.

1. The Gift of Love

l. Michalson, Carl. *The Witness of Radical Faith.* (Tennessee, 1974), p. 102.

2. Canfield, Jack and Hanson Mark Victor. *Chicken Soup of the Soul.* (Florida, 1993), pp. 3–4.

3. United Methodist Hymnal. (Tennessee, 1989) #408

2. The Gift of Kindness

1. Palacio, R.J. *Wonder.* (New York, 2012), pp. 298 -301

2. Harding, Kelli. The Rabbit Effect. (New York, 2019), pp. xxiii–xxv.

3. The Gift of Empathy

1. Quoist, Michael. *Prayers.* (New York, 1963), p. 112.

4. The Gift of Compassion

1. Armstrong, Karen. *Twelve Steps to a Compassionate Life.* (New York, 2011), pp. 9–11.

2. "What Is Compassion?" *Greater Good Magazine: Science-Based Insights for a Meaningful Life.* https://greatergood.berkeley.edu/topic/compassion/definition accessed 11/14/2021

3. Wilkerson, Isabel. *Caste.* (New York, 2020), p. 75.

4. Hershey, Terry. *This Is the Life.* (Cincinnati, 2009), p.98

5. Dalai and Desmond Tutu. *The Book of Joy.* (New York, 2006), pp. 252-257.

6. Armstrong, Karen. *Twelve Steps to a Compassionate Life.* (New York, 2011), pp. 9-11.

7. Dalai and Desmond Tutu. *The Book of Joy.* (New York, 2006), pp. 252-257.

7. The Gift of Listening

1. Raines, Robert. *Creative* Brooding. (New York, 1977).

2. "Thich Nhat Hanh on Compassionate Listening," *Super Soul Sunday* (OWN) http://cultureofempathy.com/references/Experts/Thich-Nhat-Hanh.htm accessed 11/29/2021

8. The Gift of Touch

1. McNichols, Nicole K. Ph.D., "The Vital Importance of Human Touch" https://www.psychologytoday.com/us/blog/every-one-top/202108/the-vital-importance-human-touch accessed 11/29/2021

2. "The Importance of Touching and Being Touched" https://exploringyourmind.com/the-importance-of-touching-and-being-touched/ accessed 11/29/2021

10. The Gift of Affirmation

1. Nouwen, Henri J.M. *Life of the Beloved.* (New York, 1993), pp. 58–59.

2. Ernst, Lisa. *Located in the Lion's Roar.* September Issue, 2021.

11. The Gift of Time

1. Tillich, Paul. *The New Being.* (Nebraska, 2005), pp. 46–49.

2. Thich Nhat Hanh. *The Art of Living.* (New York, 2017), p. 198.

14. The Gift of Vulnerability

1. Black, Michael Ian. *A Better Man: A (Mostly Serious) Letter to My Son.* (North Carolina, 2020), p. 104.

2. Ibid., p. 105.

3. Trebek, Alex. *The Answer Is.* (New York, 2020), p. 259.

15. The Gift of Forgiveness

1. "Making Amends," https://www.hazeldenbettyford.org/articles/making-amends-addiction-recovery accessed 11/29/2021

17. The Gift of Generosity

1. The Dalai Lama. Beyond Religion: Ethics for a Whole World. (New York, 2012), ch. 10.

18. The Gift of Legacy

1. Moore, James. W. At the End of the Day. (Nashville, 2002), pp. 7–8.

About the Author

James R. Hallam James R. Hallam has been committed to a life of service for nearly 60 years as a United Methodist minister, a dean of students, a professor, and most recently, a township supervisor. Jim believes that the roots of human fulfillment lie in our relationships with self and others and sees Jesus of Nazareth as the ultimate role model for a meaningful life on earth.

He holds a D.Min. and M.Div. from Drew University, an M.S. in Education, focusing on psychological services, from the University of Pennsylvania, and a B.A. from Dickinson College. Born and raised in Philadelphia, Jim lives in Newtown Square, PA with his wonderful wife, Kerry. Between them, they have seven adult children and one very special dog.